Discovering the Jesus

Real Questions...
REAL JESUS

χ The Greek Way to Say Jesus

For centuries it has been a symbol for Christ, the anointed one, the Savior. First-century Christians used the Greek letter χ (pronounced ki or key), which is the first letter in the Greek word for Christ, χριστός (pronounced Kree-stas) as a shorthand for Jesus. The χ quickly became incorporated into a variety of symbols to represent early Christians' faith in the one God sent, Jesus. It was simple. It pointed to the cross and became a sign identifying believers. The mark and its variation can be found in ancient Roman catacombs, early coins, lamps, and pottery.

Today, χ still stands for Christ. It is the bridge between the countless number of Christ-followers through history to a new millennium. As you prepare yourself for the future, you will need the right tools to make sense of a world that often appears senseless. You will need answers to the tough questions. You will need a firm foundation on which to make good decisions about your life and your future. You will need the χ–Jesus.

Through this devotional, *Discovering the Jesus Answers*, and its companion devotional books, *Knowing the Real Jesus, Finding the Jesus Experience*, and *Meeting the Jesus Challenge*, you will encounter the *real* Jesus and what he has to say about faith, pain and suffering, relationships, and other issues that touch your life. In this series of 30 devotions, you will discover who Jesus really is, why he came to earth, and why he deserves your trust, your worship, and your faith.

χ. One symbol. One hope. One man. One God. One Truth. It's all you'll ever need.

Discovering the Jesus Answers

Real Life...
Real Questions...
REAL JESUS

Len Woods

EMPOWERED® Youth Products

Standard Publishing
Cincinnati, Ohio

All Scripture quotations, unless otherwise indicated, are taken from the *Holy Bible,* New Living Translation, copyright © 1996. Used by permission of Tyndale House Publishers, Inc., Wheaton, IL 60189. All rights reserved.

Developed and produced for Standard Publishing by The Livingstone Corporation. Project staff includes: Kirk Luttrell, Andrea Reider, Betsy Todt Schmitt, Ashley Taylor, and David R. Veerman.

Some material included in *Discovering the Jesus Answers* was used by permission from *The Jesus Bible*, copyright ©2002 by Tyndale House Publishers, Inc. All rights reserved.

Contributing writers include: Mark Fackler, Amber Hudson, Randy Southern, Linda Washington, and Neil Wilson.

Standard Publishing development and editorial team includes: Paul Learned, Darrell Lewis, Dale Reeves, acquisitions editor, and Mark Taylor.

Cover design, Ahaa! Design

Interior design, Kirk Luttrell, The Livingstone Corporation

Library of Congress Cataloging-in-Publication Data:
Woods, Len, 1958-
    Discovering the Jesus answers / Len Woods.
        p.   cm. – (Real life – real questions – real Jesus)
    ISBN 0-7847-1425-8 (pbk.)
  1. Theology, Doctrinal–popular works.   2. Youth–Prayer-books and devotions–English. I. Title. II. Series.
    BT77 .W66 2002
    230–dc21
                                      2002008145

EMPOWERED® Youth Products is a trademark of Standard Publishing.

Printed in the United States of America.

Standard Publishing, Cincinnati, Ohio.

A Division of Standex International Corporation.

09 08 07 06 05 04 03 02

7 6 5 4 3 2 1

Contents

The Jesus Experience

The *Real Life … Real Questions … Real Jesus* series, consisting of four devotional books and four leader's guides for youth leaders, were written as companion pieces to *The Jesus Bible*. This Bible, published by Tyndale Publishing House and produced and developed by The Livingstone Corporation, was designed to help introduce the Jesus of the Bible to you in a new and fresh way. *The Jesus Bible* follows the work and purpose of Christ from the Old Testament prophecies about him to his life and ministry on earth. It records Jesus' call to radical living, first voiced about 2,000 years ago, that still resounds today.

Through the features and notes found in *The Jesus Bible*, you will encounter Jesus in ways you have never experienced before—not the watered-down religious pacifist or the timid-looking person in a stained-glass window. But the Christ, the Messiah, the Savior, the real Jesus—in all his color, with all his power, showing up in the most unexpected places and taking the most revolutionary actions. Through *The Jesus Bible*, you will meet the real Jesus for real life with real answers for life's tough problems.

Why the New Living Translation?

Since its inception, Tyndale House Publishing has been committed to publishing editions of the Bible in the language of the common people. With more than 40 million copies in print, *The Living Bible* represented this tradition for more than 30 years. In recent years, Tyndale continued its commitment and mission by commissioning 90 evangelical scholars to produce the *Holy Bible*, New Living Translation. This general-purpose translation is accurate and excellent for study, yet it is easy to read and understand.

The team of translators was challenged to create a text that would have the same impact in the lives of modern readers as the original text did in the lives of early believers. To accomplish that, the team translated entire thoughts (rather than just words) into natural, everyday

English. The result is a translation that speaks to us today in our language, a translation that is easy to understand, and that accurately communicates the meaning of the original texts.

In using the New Living Translation for *The Jesus Bible* and in the *Real Life ... Real Questions ... Real Jesus* series, the publishers at Tyndale House and Standard Publishing pray that this translation will speak to your heart and help you understand the Word of God in a fresh and powerful way.

Because you have real questions ...
and Jesus has real answers!

Corrie ten Boom was a woman well-acquainted with evil. Imprisoned by the Nazis in 1940s Germany, Corrie had a ringside seat to the Holocaust.

SUFFERING AND EVIL

You would think seeing so much cruelty and suffering would turn a heart hard. You'd expect such a horrifying ordeal to shatter someone's faith, not strengthen it. Yet Corrie ten Boom emerged from this darkest of human experiences with a vibrant trust in the goodness of God. In her own words: "When a train goes through a tunnel and it gets dark, you don't throw away the ticket and jump off. You sit still and trust the engineer."

These first eight devotions are all about the dark "tunnel" times of your life, and how and why you should trust the great Engineer of the universe.

DaY 1

I discover the Jesus Answer when I trust in the hope found in him no matter what my circumstances.

"But not a hair of your head will perish! By standing firm, you will win your souls."

Luke 21:18-19

REAL Xpressions

The Problem of Evil

My mom says I'll always re-member the details of 9-11. Just like she will never forget exactly where she was and what she was doing the day the Space Shuttle exploded.

I'm pretty sure she's right. I was in study hall, doodling, thinking about the weekend, about Mark, about whatever, and suddenly Mrs. Babinger came rushing in the room. She looked terrified, pale. Flipping on the TV, she said, to nobody and everybody, "We're under attack!"

For the next 45 minutes we all just sat there, numb, staring, watching. Nobody said much of anything. Over and over we saw replays of the second jet slamming into the second tower. Then came reports from the Pentagon. Reporters speculating about it all. And then, of course, those awful moments when the towers just collapsed. I'm not usually an emotional person, and I hate for people to see me cry. But that morning I didn't care. And I didn't even try to fight back the tears.

All this time later, even if I close my eyes, I can still see it all vividly. The images just won't go away.

I guess it's true what some people say. Everything changed that day. Everything. The world will never be the same. And if I'm honest, my faith changed too. I don't mean I stopped believing in God. I guess I mean I started questioning more. It's like my eyes were opened to the reality of evil. Before it always seemed remote, far away, sort of like a vague concept. Now it's so close to home. And it has a face.

Right now I just want to know if my faith in Christ offers any satisfying answers as to why this kind of thing can happen.

Stacey

REAL QUESTION

It's the classic, age-old question. It's the dilemma that has puzzled philosophers and stumped theologians for ages: Why is there evil in the world?

No doubt you've asked it yourself. It's hard to reconcile the claim that God is perfectly wise, totally good, and absolutely powerful in the world we inhabit. Doesn't it seem like an all-wise, all-powerful God could have designed a world free of evil? Doesn't it seem like a completely good God would have done so?

Yet, we live in a world where really bad stuff happens and where darkness often seems to win. Stacey's question is legitimate: Does the Christian faith offer any answers to the question of evil? Like Stacey, when we close our eyes we can still see the images. Not just the madmen slamming their planes into the World Trade Center. But starving orphans in AIDS-ravaged Africa. Hitler's death camps. The innocent faces of the victims of a serial killer.

REAL ANSWER

Evil in this world is a fact of life. Period. Jesus plainly told his disciples that they would suffer: "There will be a time of great persecution. You will be dragged into synagogues and prisons, and you will be accused before kings and governors of being my followers" (Luke 21:12). But, Jesus concluded, *"Not a hair of your head will perish"* (Luke 21:18). What was Jesus talking about? We know that Peter was martyred as were many of the other disciples. Countless others have died for their faith over the years. Jesus was not promising his disciples (present and past) that they would be forever protected from the consequences of evil. Rather, Jesus was saying that his followers would never suffer spiritual or eternal loss. Ultimately, our hope is found in heaven through Christ.

The question still nags at us, however: Why, God? Why? How could you let such things happen? Why do you stand by and do nothing?

The answer, while not terribly complicated, is unsettling. When God created man, he didn't program his creatures to mindlessly obey. And still he refuses to *force* anyone to love him. God lets his human creatures choose. And from the very beginning this risky setup has resulted in bad, wrong, selfish, and devastating choices. Adam and Eve, the first human creatures, stubbornly chose to reject God's perfect plan for their lives and try to find life and meaning apart from their Creator. The result of these choices has been a flood of wickedness. Not only is the human heart filled with evil (Jeremiah 17:9), but the whole world is consumed with evil (Romans 1–3).

Jesus has already instituted a plan to overcome evil. This plan included the cross and the resurrection, and it set into motion a series of events that are unstoppable. God will bring a final end to evil at the perfect time of his choosing, a time still in the future. This is the Christian hope: that God is so wise and perfect and loving, that he can cause even this evil world system to end in the greatest possible glory for himself and the greatest possible joy for those who trust him.

As believers, we cling to this hope that is found in Jesus. Because he lived, because he suffered, because he died, and then, because he rose again, we have hope that one day Jesus will return and one day, we will be in heaven with him. Admittedly, such explanations, no matter how sound, can't erase grief. Talk of the eventual destruction of evil does nothing about the reality of evil now. But hope is a huge and necessary part of the healing process.

REAL YOU

With human freedom comes the potential for great evil. But such a design also opens a door for great good. Some wonderful and positive things in the world are:

_____

_____

_____

_____

_____

_____

_____

_____

I can't erase all the evil in the world, but I can act. And I won't let my inability to do everything keep me from doing *something*. Specifically, I will commit to combat evil by taking the following steps:

_____

_____

_____

_____

_____

_____

_____

_____

Χalted

Hope

The Bible doesn't use the word "hope" as we so often do. To us, it usually means we're not sure about something or we sense there's a strong chance something we desire will *not* come to pass. In the Bible, "hope" is strong confidence and unwavering trust in the promises of God. As the Christian's ultimate hope (1 Timothy 1:1), Jesus gives the assurance that he will see us through whatever hard times may come. Jesus *is* our assurance that ultimately we will share in his eternal glory (Colossians 1:27).

DAY 2

I discover the Jesus Answer when I trust that God completely understands my suffering.

Jesus wept.

John 11:35

REAL XPRESSIONS

Whispers and Tears

Most people are pretty good at holding things together on the outside. In public they appear to be OK— externally there might even be smiles and a seemingly normal routine.

Take my best friend Lauren, for example. To see her walk through the hallways, smiling and talking with her friends, practicing her gymnastic routine with the rest of the team each day after school, and complaining about homework, you would never know that anything is wrong.

Behind closed doors, though, everything changes. The brave front melts. The façade crumbles. Because I'm close enough and trusted enough, I see the tears. I hear the pain in her voice. I hold her as she shakes with anger and fear. I was the first to know.

A few weeks ago Lauren went out with this guy, a guy who's really cute and popular in school. Well, anyway, to make a long story short, he got her drunk. Or maybe he drugged her. And then he raped her. Lauren's scared to death. And humiliated. And incredibly sad. I'm the only person she's told. I keep telling her to go to the police, but there's no way she's gonna do that. She says her parents would never understand; it would absolutely devastate them. So she's trying to handle it herself.

I don't get it. Lauren was so committed to saving herself for marriage. Why her? She was totally innocent. She trusted that guy, you know. She *trusted* him!

Every time I see this guy in class or after school, I want to scream at him. And every time I see Lauren, I want to cry and just hold on to her and let her know everything is going to be all right. And pray for her. It's all I know to do.

Rachel

REAL QUESTION

The fact of suffering, whether the result of natural disaster or (like the stories above) the evil of humanity, is confusing. When life gets really ugly, and the pain is intolerable, where is God? Why does he seem to just stand by while the innocent suffer?

Doesn't he care? Can *anything* good possibly come from a star athlete's blown-out knee? A debilitating illness? A horrific crime? The death of a marriage, a dream, or a loved one?

You may not be wrestling with a heavy issue such as Lauren experienced (and here's a prayer that you'll never have to), but somewhere along the line, you *will* crash head-on into the reality of suffering. In one way or another, it will hunt you down. And then you'll experience the bitter pain of living in a world very nearly ruined by creatures who have dismissed and despised their Creator.

What will you do? What would you say if the whispered secrets in the previous story were coming from one of *your* friends?

REAL ANSWER

The fact of *evil* (see the previous devotional) leads to the universal reality of *suffering.* Pain, sadness, grief, mourning, tears, hunger, emptiness—all this is the human condition. Happiness, laughter, comfort—we enjoy these things to be sure, but given the promise of an all-powerful, perfectly good God, we wonder why bad times come at all, much less stay with us for such long, excruciating periods.

This is the great mystery, the universal question: Where is God when his creatures are in pain? Well, we do know where Jesus was when Mary and Martha were grieving the loss of their brother, Lazarus. He was right there with them . . . in the cemetery . . . weeping.

The consistent testimony of the Bible is that God sees our troubles (Genesis 16:13; Psalm 33:13) and hears our cries (Psalm 34:17; 55:17; 69:33). He is never unaware of our pain or indifferent to our suffering. On the contrary, our pain pains him (Exodus 2:23-25). We know, too, that Jesus experienced many emotions—compassion, anger, sorrow, frustration. He often expressed deep emotion, as evident in his encounter with the two sisters (John 11:33-38).

So why then does God stand by and allow the hurt to go on and on? Maybe for the same reason that he stood by when vicious, cruel men spit in the face of his Son, when they beat him senseless, when they cursed and mocked him, and when they hammered him to a Roman cross. Never was one more innocent. And yet God refused to intervene. Why?

What is God doing? What is he up to? Maybe what the Bible says is true. Perhaps in allowing pain, God is doing something profound. Maybe he *is* showing the universe that there is nothing so terrible and ugly that he cannot turn it to good. Maybe the most grotesque actions will actually give way in time (certainly in eternity) to the most glorious results. Maybe through suffering our character can be transformed in ways we never imagined. Maybe if we handle suffering right, we become the most powerful witnesses possible. Maybe the trick is on Satan, and God really *will* get the last laugh.

This much we know: When we find ourselves in the flood or in the fire, Jesus says he is there with us (Psalm 23; Isaiah 43:2; Daniel 3:19-25; Hebrews 13:5). *We never* go through suffering alone. And when we can't sense his presence, we have the tangible, visible body of Christ—the church (that is, our fellow Christians)—to lean upon for the encouragement and strength to keep going.

And we have the promise that at some point, the pain *will* stop. We have God's word on that (Psalm 30:5; 66:12).

REAL YOU

When my friends are hurting, I will resist the urge to offer "pat answers" and instead I will do the following:

_____

_____

_____

_____

_____

_____

_____

_____

_____

_____

_____

_____

When I am suffering I will strive to remember the following truths about Jesus:

_____

_____

_____

_____

_____

_____

_____

_____

_____

_____

_____

_____

_____

Xalted

Light of the World

When we find ourselves in a
dark or scary place what we want
and need most is light. When we face
those dark and scary times of life, Jesus is
our self-proclaimed "light of the world" (John
8:12). He illumines the path we need to take, giving
us hope and guidance.

DAY I discover the Jesus Answer when I focus on God's perspective on suffering and evil rather than my own.

Then Jesus began to tell them that he, the Son of Man, would suffer many terrible things and be rejected by the leaders, the leading priests, and the teachers of religious law. He would be killed, and three days later he would rise again. As he talked about this openly with his disciples, Peter took him aside and told him he shouldn't say things like that.

Jesus turned and looked at his disciples and then said to Peter very sternly, "Get away from me, Satan! You are seeing things merely from a human point of view, not from God's."

Mark 8:31-33

REAL Xpressions

Suffering Servants

We had this missionary come speak at our church yesterday. As a matter of fact, this guy and my Dad are old friends. They went to college together and were even roommates for a year or so.

Now, normally I *hate* missionary speakers. I don't know why. I guess I feel like they're so outdated. You know, like they've been in a time warp and they just popped in from the 1970s or something. And they're usually so stern and grim. You feel like you're being lectured, like you should feel guilty because you have a North American zip code.

Eric and his wife were *nothing* like that. They came and ate lunch with us after church. I'm telling you they were *hilarious!* Cute, well-behaved kids too. Just happy little campers. The whole time Eric kept telling these amazing stories from their seven years of working with Muslims in Macedonia. Life is pretty hard there. And being a Christian is downright dangerous. Some of their stories were almost as wild as the stuff you read about in the Bible with the apostle Paul.

Anyway, here's what gets me: Eric could have stayed *here,* made a nice salary, and enjoyed a comfy life. Instead he drags his family halfway around the world to serve Jesus, to spread the gospel. Here's a guy—a whole family!—radically committed to Christ. And what do they have to show for it?

Well, the doctors think Eric has some kind of incurable liver disease—probably from a dirty needle doctors used on him in some foreign hospital. And the family has serious financial concerns (in fact, one reason they were here is that if they can't raise more funds, they'll have to come home for good). They've got one set of parents who won't even speak to them because they don't want their grandkids overseas. And, the biggest blow of all, two of Eric's most influential Muslim converts were recently killed. Eric had spent three years preparing these guys to lead the church there. Now all that effort seems lost.

I don't get it. It's like in every way, Eric keeps getting knocked down. He just wants to serve God. You would think God would give him a break.

Luke

REAL QUESTION

Admit it. You've had the same thought. Shouldn't Christians get a break? Shouldn't we be exempt? Don't faith and obedience count for something? Doesn't God take care of his own? Common sense says you *reward* your friends, not *punish* them. Yet in God's way of doing things, the situation often seems reversed! Look at all that Eric has gone through!

From a public relations perspective, isn't this a crazy way for God to try to "grow his Church"? How many people are going to want to put their faith in Jesus if the Christians all around them are constantly struggling?

REAL answer

In a world where suffering abounds (and wrong ideas *about* suffering flourish), it's super important for us think correctly. We *have* to remember the things that God has said.

This is a fallen world. Our whole creation suffers (Romans 8:22) from the curse of Eden (Genesis 3:14-19). It's because of the great rebellion there that evil, pain, and sadness exist. Add to this the fact that our great enemy, the devil, is a cruel and hateful creature who is bent on causing as much misery and destruction as he possibly can (1 Peter 5:8-9). The result is a world marred and scarred by sin. Every human is affected.

The bad news, as Jesus put it, is that in this world we will have trouble (John 16:33). The good news is that Christ—at the cross—has already taken away sin's *penalty* and *power.* Not only that, but the day is coming when he will take his children away from sin's very *presence.*

No one is exempt from suffering. God doesn't play favorites. Even the faithful go through hard times. Look at the Old Testament men, like Abraham and Jacob. Consider Job. Read the psalms of David (almost as many desperate pleas there as hymns of praise!). Study the prophets. Trace the life of the apostles. All of them suffered greatly. And Christians still do. Did you know more believers in Jesus were killed for their faith in the 20th century than in the previous 19 centuries combined?

The facts are clear: Enlisting in God's army isn't some kind of guarantee of a pain-free life. On the contrary, when we declare allegiance to Christ, we declare ourselves Satan's enemies. We might as well paint a big target on our chest!

We believe in Jesus and follow him, not because of what we might get (or think we might avoid), but because he is the truth.

God is able to bring good out of our suffering. Suffering builds character (Romans 5:3-5). Suffering forces us to hold on to God. Suffering draws Christians together. Suffering (if handled correctly) draws others to Christ. These are *bad* things?

Suffering will one day cease. The great promise of Revelation 21 and 22 is of a "new heaven and new earth" in which death, pain, and mourning will be no more. The whole world will be made new, and we will enjoy the very presence of God. Read these fascinating chapters and thank God for the great future that awaits the faithful followers of Christ.

Knowing these facts doesn't make suffering fun—for Eric or any other believer. But trusting in these truths can change our outlook and give us the strength to keep going during life's toughest times.

REAL YOU

Suffering is a fact of life in a fallen world—even for believers. I can either run from this truth or embrace it. The truth from this lesson I need to remember the most is:

_____

_____

_____

_____

_____

_____

_____

_____

_____

_____

_____

_____

_____

If I let him, God will use hard times in my life to accomplish his glory and my good. Here are the difficulties in my life that I will ask God, not to take away, but to use for his purposes:

_____

_____

_____

_____

_____

_____

_____

_____

_____

_____

_____

_____

_____

_____

_____

_____

_____

_____

_____

_____

Χalted

Angel of His Presence

Many Bible scholars believe
the Old Testament appearances of
the "angel of the Lord" are really instances where Jesus showed up (before his
earthly birth). This is likely the thought in
Isaiah 63:9 where we find a reference to the "angel
of his presence" (NIV). (See also Exodus 23:20-23, NLT.)
The point? Christ was right there when his people were in trouble. And he's also right there with you when *you* hurt.

DAY

I discover the Jesus Answer when I honestly face my own problems and difficulties.

"And you will know the truth, and the truth will set you free."
John 8:32

REAL Xpressions

Morning, Noon, and Night

Naiya lost a lot of weight last summer. She was always really cute, but now she's a stick. I knew she'd been running a lot, so I just assumed she'd lost weight because of that. I didn't suspect anything was wrong.

But when you live with a roommate and share the same bathroom, you notice little things. Naiya always went to the bathroom right after she ate. Her eyes were often bloodshot, as if she'd broken a blood vessel in them somehow. I noticed strands of her hair everywhere and those telltale signs around the toilet rim. Naiya's secret was out. I can't believe I didn't catch on sooner.

For months I watched my friend wrestle with this brutal condition called bulimia. At times I felt helpless and sad. On other occasions I felt angry at her for doing this to herself. I tried to drop hints to her and bring it up, but she wouldn't acknowledge it. She just denied she had a problem.

Not knowing what else to do, I prayed. Every day. All the time. That was eight months ago.

Her mom finally noticed the problem, thank goodness, just as I prayed she would. Over the summer, when Naiya was back at home, her mom made her meet with a Christian counselor and a nutritionist every week. She forced Naiya to face her problem.

I got this letter from Naiya last week, and for the first time, she admitted her struggle. Here's what the last little bit says:

My mom reminded me that God cares how I treat my body. She said that he knows how hard meal times are for me, now that I'm trying to eat healthy again. She wrote this verse on a card for me, and I carry it with me all the time:

> *"Morning, noon, and night*
> *I plead aloud in my distress,*
> *and the Lord hears my voice."*

Morning, noon, and night—the three times a day when I eat— I ask God to help me eat healthy, and he hears my voice. Keep praying for me, OK, Holli? See you soon.

Love,

Naiya

Holli

REAL QUESTION

For Naiya, her great struggle in life is an eating disorder. For your friends, it could be that, or it might be any number of other concerns: academic problems, difficulty on the home front, relationship nightmares, or financial trouble.

As you mentally run through the names and faces in your life, does it seem to you that certain people have it made? Ever know anyone who seems to have the perfect, problem-free life? Why do you think so many people feel pressured to deny they have problems and to pretend all is OK?

What about you? In what ways do *you* struggle and how do you cope? Are you quick to discuss your problems with others? Why or why not?

Real answer

The Old Testament book of Ecclesiastes, penned by King Solomon, offers a very sobering, some would say "cynical" look at the world. In the course of this somewhat depressing message, Solomon accurately describes what it feels like to live in a fallen world. Consider how he describes the human condition:

- "So what do people get for all their hard work? Their days of labor are filled with pain and grief; even at night they cannot rest. It is all utterly meaningless" (2:22-23).
- "I observed all the oppression that takes place in our world. I saw the tears of the oppressed, with no one to comfort them. The oppressors have great power, and the victims are helpless. So I concluded that the dead are better off than the living. And most fortunate of all are those who were never born. For they have never seen all the evil that is done in our world" (4:1-3).
- "In this meaningless life, I have seen everything, including the fact that some good people die young and some wicked people live on and on" (7:15).
- "I have thought deeply about all that goes on here in the world, where people have the power to hurt each other." (8:9).

And on and on it goes.

We can take issue with Solomon's bleak tone and call him a pessimist, but we cannot deny his main point: The world is filled with pain and heartache, and *no one* is exempt from suffering. The plain fact is the world is a mess and people are broken. We *all* are. Each of us fails and hurts. We struggle, if not in one area, then in another. So why do we try to pretend? Why do we feel compelled to act as though things are better than they are?

Understand this is not a call to wallow in our pain and to feel sorry for ourselves. It is simply a challenge to be honest and real. To courageously acknowledge the struggles in our lives and then, with God's help (and the encouragement of other believers), to deal with them. Paul did not deny the reality of his so-called "thorn in the flesh" (2 Corinthians 12), but he also didn't have a pity party. He faced up to it, and kept walking in faith.

So long as we deny what's true, we play into the hands of the evil one, who Jesus called "the father of lies" (John 8:44). On the other hand, when we own up to the truth of our own struggles and begin telling the truth about our lives, we experience unearthly freedom (John 8:32). The pressure is suddenly off to pretend. And realizing that everyone else has problems too, we find greater compassion within our hearts.

REAL YOU

Because I am tired of trying to appear as though I have it all together, I will take the following three steps:

_____

_____

_____

_____

_____

_____

_____

_____

_____

_____

_____

_____

_____

_____

_____

_____

Some practical ways I can help my friends move through their pain and struggles are:

_____

_____

_____

_____

_____

_____

_____

_____

_____

_____

_____

_____

_____

_____

Χalted

Immanuel

The prophet Isaiah foretold of a coming Savior who would be "Immanuel" (Isaiah 7:14)–literally meaning "God with us." Sure enough, the eternal God took on flesh and came and lived among us as Jesus Christ (John 1:1, 14). This astounding fact means, among other things, that Jesus understands the struggles of humanity and that he has compassion for a hurting human race.

I discover the Jesus Answer when I accept the fact that living for Christ may involve suffering.

"Then you will be arrested, persecuted, and killed. You will be hated all over the world because of your allegiance to me."

Matthew 24:9

REAL Xpressions

A Bad Rep

Girls at my school have a choice. You can either be popular with the girls or popular with the guys. You can't do both, because if guys like you too much, then the girls won't like you at all. That's just the way it is.

Darien found that out the hard way when she moved here in the fall. She has the kind of personality that guys drool over–funny and a little flirty. And did I mention that she looks like a model? No wonder she always has three or four guys around her no matter where she goes.

It's also no wonder that at any given moment she has at least three or four girls talking about her behind her back. Some of them really *hate* her. I'm not even going to tell you what they say about her. It's obvious they're just jealous. They can't stand that she gets more attention than they do. So they're always trying to find things wrong with her.

I don't really know Darien that well, but every time I've talked to her she's seemed really sweet. She's not conceited at all. And when I see her with guys, they're usually just joking around or talking about school stuff. I don't think she's the kind of person everyone thinks she is.

If I tell anyone that, though, I might as well paint a big target on my back because pretty soon people will be talking about me, too.

But if that's the way it has to be, fine. I made a decision to live for Christ, and a big part of that is loving other people. If that means I have to sacrifice my own popularity (what little I have) to stand up for Darien, I'll do it.

Sandy

REAL QUESTION

Ever been in a situation
like the one Sandy describes?
What did you do? What happened?
What advice would you give to her if she
asked your counsel?

An old chorus talks about the cost of following
Jesus, and one of its verses says, "Though none go with
me, still I will follow." Easy to sing, but tough to do—it's a
vow to go against the whole world if necessary, to do the right
thing even if no one else does.

Why do you think it is so tough to stand up for what is right?

Could you break with all your friends if you had to? Would you have
the guts to deliberately choose an unpopular path that might lead to
weird looks or even harsh words?

REAL ANSWER

Christians have a tenden-
cy to focus mostly on the positive statements of Scripture. We
buy books filled with encouraging Bible
promises. We hang framed needlepoint bless-
ings on our living room walls. We are quick to memorize passages like "the prayer of Jabez" (1 Chronicles
4:10), verses that speak of God's extravagant goodness to his
children.

But it's also important for us to remember some of God's less-than-
thrilling promises. When's the last time you pondered these statements
from the lips of Jesus:

- Matthew 24:9: "Then you will be arrested, persecuted, and killed. You
  will be hated all over the world because of your allegiance to me." (And
  indeed all over the world, as you are reading this sentence, some 200
  million Christians are in very real danger of being arrested, persecuted, and killed!)

- John 15:18: "When the world hates you, remember it hated me before it hated you." (Notice Jesus says there "when" the world hates you, not "if" it does! He goes on to say in verse 20 of this same chapter, "Since they persecuted me, naturally they will persecute you.")

What's the point? The point is exactly what the apostle discovered and declared, "everyone who wants to live a godly life in Christ Jesus will suffer persecution" (2 Timothy 3:12).

If Sandy bucks the crowd of jealous girls and opts instead to treat Darien with love and kindness, she will take the heat. And you, every time you stand for what is right, will be opening yourself up to attack.

If sinful people killed the prophets and tried to silence the apostles, people will certainly try to make your life miserable. Those in darkness can't stand the light of truth and righteousness. They try to extinguish it or at the very least discredit it.

Suffering for doing right hurts as much as any other kind of suffering. But at least we know we're in good company. And we have one more promise from Christ: "God blesses you when you are mocked and persecuted and lied about because you are my followers. Be happy about it! Be very glad! For a great reward awaits you in heaven" (Matthew 5:11-12).

Real you

On a scale of 1-10 (with 1 meaning "I *never* face persecution" and 10 representing "I've got people in my life who want to *crucify* me because of my faith in Christ") how would you rate your current Christian experience and why?

_____

_____

_____

_____

_____

_____

How does it make you feel to know that God pledges to reward those who stay the course—and refuse to compromise their convictions?

_____

_____

_____

_____

_____

_____

_____

_____

_____

_____

_____

_____

_____

_____

_____

_____

_____

_____

_____

_____

_____

_____

XALTED

Head Shepherd

If you were a poor, defenseless sheep surrounded by wolves, wouldn't you want to know that a good and strong shepherd was guarding your woolen hide? Guess what? You *are* a spiritual sheep in a wolf-filled world. Jesus is the ultimate shepherd, the head Shepherd (1 Peter 5:4), who stands at your side. Relax. You may catch some heat for belonging to him, but in the ultimate, eternal sense, you are 100% safe.

DAY 6

I discover the Jesus Answer when I accept suffering as a consequence of my wrong choices.

"You have heard that the law of Moses says, 'Do not murder. If you commit murder, you are subject to judgment.' But I say, if you are angry with someone, you are subject to judgment! If you call someone an idiot, you are in danger of being brought before the high council. And if you curse someone, you are in danger of the fires of hell."

Matthew 5:21-22

REAL Xpressions

Painful Consequences!

I really don't have any excuse.
None at all. It was a dumb thing,
spur of the moment. I panicked, and
now I'm paying a stiff price.

But even if my actions are inexcusable, they're understandable. At least I think so. See, Mrs. Todd is the toughest teacher at my school—heck, maybe even the whole world. She's legendary for her pop tests, impossible term papers, and tough grading. It's like she takes pleasure in watching her students sweat and squirm and barely squeak by.

Last Friday, she did it again. A surprise, short essay on the poetry of William Blake. I knew with progress reports coming out, I couldn't afford to flag another assignment.

Well, would you believe Mrs. Todd got called to the office? Before leaving she warned us about not cheating, but the minute she was out the door, *everyone* started grabbing lecture notes and textbooks. I don't think half the class even knew who William Blake was!

I just got caught up in the moment. And I wasn't very good at covering my tracks.

That night, Mrs. Todd recognized some of my phrases as coming right out of our class notes (Doesn't this woman have a life?). Bam. I was nailed—the *only* person nailed. The next day she called me into her office and went ballistic, and as much as I wanted to say, "Hey, everybody did it!" I just bit my tongue.

So, not only do I get an "F" (actually a zero!) for that test, but Mrs. Todd is also talking possible suspension.

My mom is furious. She keeps asking, "Why? Why?" And what can I say to that? "Gee, Mom, I guess you have an idiot for a son."

Last night, I was reading through Psalms, and Psalm 38 caught my attention. I'm not sure what David did wrong, but he was obviously in hot water. He admitted his sin and cried out to God for rescue.

Right now, I don't know what else to do.

Estevan

REAL QUESTION

Maybe you have been where Estevan is in the situation above. What a mess! What did you do? How would you advise him? Should he have ratted on his class, or is that really the issue?

Should his focus be on all the others who "got away with cheating," or should he mostly be concerned with his own actions?

What lessons can we learn from Estevan's poor choices?

REAL ANSWER

Much of our suffering is self-induced. Not always. Sometimes, as we do the right thing, we get persecuted. Occasionally we're minding our own business when calamity comes and whacks us over the head. (See Jesus' comments in John 9:3.) But Jesus also reminded his followers that instances also arise when we do wrong, we get caught, and we pay the price. (See Matthew 5:21-22, for example.) It's that simple.

That's the reality Estevan is face-to-face with. And if we're wise, we'll learn from Estevan's situation (and save ourselves a ton of grief).

One truth is that nobody gets away with anything (at least not in the ultimate sense). Everybody gets caught eventually. The Bible says, without qualification, that we reap what we sow (Galatians 6:7-8). There *is* a payday. Estevan's classmates may think they skated, but they are messing with the indisputable laws of the universe. You can't cheat God. You can't violate his standards and escape the consequences. Not for very long, anyway.

A second truth from Estevan's story is that God disciplines his children (Hebrews 12). Like a good parent, God corrects Christians when they get out of line. These trips to the woodshed can take many forms: an illness, a financial setback, or an academic problem, for example. But the fact is that sometimes God allows (or even brings) certain unpleasant experiences in our lives because he loves us. He wants to train us to do right. He wants us to avoid activities and habits that will cause us even further grief down the road. What kind of parent would God be if he just let us run wild and he never corrected us?

A third truth is that disobedience is painful. Estevan's situation may get worse before it gets better. And though God is quick to forgive us, he doesn't usually take away the consequences of our wrong choices.

Fourth, getting caught and being disciplined by God is actually a blessing. It is God's mercy in your life, God's way of trying to flag you down, get your attention, and get you to turn around before you get in worse trouble.

The penalty for Estevan now might be suspension. But that's nothing compared to the classmate who foolishly thinks he can continue to get away with cheating and who one day will end up in the slammer. In the words of Proverbs 6:23: "The correction of discipline is the way to life."

real you

Some painful times in
my life when I suffered
because of my own wrong
choices are:

_____

_____

_____

_____

_____

_____

_____

_____

_____

_____

_____

_____

_____

_____

_____

_____

_____

_____

_____

A strategy that can help me avoid self-induced suffering is to take the following three steps:

_____

_____

_____

_____

_____

_____

_____

_____

_____

_____

_____

_____

Xalted

Everlasting Father

Every good father loves his children. He wants only their best. He recognizes that sometimes love must be tough. It must include confronting and correcting misbehavior. Like the ultimate father (Isaiah 9:6), Jesus is not afraid to call us on the carpet and hold us responsible for our wrong attitudes and actions. He does not delight in our suffering, but he will certainly use the pain of discipline in our lives to make us like himself. Hebrews 5:8 says even Jesus "learned obedience from the things he suffered."

I discover the Jesus Answer when I understand that *all* people will face the judgment of Christ.

"For I, the Son of Man, will come in the glory of my Father with his angels and will judge all people according to their deeds."

Matthew 16:27

REAL XPRESSIONS

Getting Away with Murder?

My town is really small (population about 8,000) and really close-knit. And right now, we are all reeling, like never before. The reason? Four high school students were buried this week—victims of a drunk driver.

The pain is indescribable. People are inconsolable. But to make matters worse, the 25-year-old man responsible for the students' deaths had been cited *three* times in the last four years for driving while intoxicated. This was the man's *fourth* offense, but because he's from a wealthy, prominent family, he has always managed to avoid jail time, getting off each time by paying a large fine and agreeing to enter an alcohol rehab center. (Some good that did!)

Now comes the shocking news that understandably angry police on the scene that grisly night may have "violated the defendant's civil and constitutional rights." There is talk that the district judge may throw out the case because of legal technicalities. In other words, an obviously guilty man, the person responsible for the senseless deaths of four kids— *four of my friends*—four great guys who everyone knew and liked, may go free.

Can you believe that?

When I really think about it, I can hardly breathe, I get so angry. If they let that &#\$@% go, there is no justice in this world! He's a *#^%@ drunk who keeps getting behind the wheel. And every time he does he endangers everyone else's life. And now he's gone and snuffed out the lives of a bunch of teens who had everything to live for! They were just out having fun. Minding their own business. And *nothing's* gonna happen to him?! No punishment at all?! That's the biggest &$%@ crime of all! If he walks, I think they ought to put the *&#^% judge in jail!

Karl

REAL QUESTION

Wow. Karl's got quite a mouth, huh? Even so, you can certainly understand his anger. We see similar incidents in our society all the time. A no-good, dirty, low-life (but rich) thug breaks the law. Very quickly whether the defendant actually committed the crime or not, the case gets lost in a sea of objections, motions, and appeals. And even when the state's case is strong, a high-priced lawyer (or whole team of attorneys) can, through various legal means and maneuvering, get their client off, or at the very least, delay justice indefinitely.

Circumstances like these raise the question, as the Bible puts it, "Why do the wicked prosper?" Why do bad people so often "get away with murder" (sometimes literally)?

REAL ANSWER

Books of the Bible like Habakkuk and passages like Psalm 73 remind us of the important truth that *no one* escapes ultimate judgment.

There's no way. God promises to punish evil, and there's no ducking God's court docket. Bad people must eventually come before the perfect judge of the universe. Once there, slick attorneys, political connections and bulging bank accounts don't matter. In that ultimate courtroom, no one can buy off the jury or plea-bargain or appeal the verdict. Eventually, the guilty get what's coming to them. Jesus declared in Matthew 16:27, "For I, the Son of Man, will come in the glory of my Father with his angels and will judge all people according to their deeds."

But this certainty poses two huge problems. First: "Eventually" is not soon enough, for many people. God's justice can seem slow to arrive, or absent altogether. The Bible itself is full of disturbed victims wondering why the bad guys prosper (that was the prophet Habakkuk's question; see 1:2-4). Nevertheless, make no mistake, God will render a just, incontestable decision, and woe to those who face it.

Second problem: We're *all* guilty. Nobody can claim total innocence. Fortunately few people murder, but tragically, we all violate God's standards in countless ways (see Romans 3:10-12, 23). We're all subject to the same sentence, which in God's plan is revoked because Jesus Christ paid the price for all who want pardon.

The next time you hear about an unfair legal decision, pause and thank God. Seriously. Thank him first for the great truth that he is utterly just (Psalm 7:17; 71:16). And then thank him second for the amazing, undeserved gift of forgiveness made possible by Christ's death on the cross. Jesus went there for *you*. He took *your* place. He hung there for *your* crimes. Only because of him can any of us avoid an eternal death sentence.

REAL YOU

It's easy to get self-righteous and all fired up about guilty people who aren't going to have to pay for their crimes. But then I have to look in the mirror. Here are some of the ways Jesus has pardoned me:

_____

_____

_____

_____

_____

_____

_____

Some friends who are struggling with the pain of earthly injustice and some practical ways I can help them are:

_____

_____

_____

_____

_____

_____

_____

_____

_____

_____

_____

_____

_____

_____

_____

_____

χALTED

Faithful and True

In John's vision of Christ (see Revelation 19:11), the aging apostle glimpses a figure on a white horse, a fair judge named "Faithful and True." This is none other than Jesus Christ! What a comfort to know that history is in his hands and that he will one day make every wrong thing right.

DAY 8

I discover the Jesus Answer when I continue to trust in him although he seems far away from me.

Eight days later the disciples were together again, and this time Thomas was with them. The doors were locked; but suddenly, as before, Jesus was standing among them. He said, "Peace be with you." Then he said to Thomas, "Put your finger here and see my hands. Put your hand into the wound in my side. Don't be faithless any longer. Believe!"

"My Lord and my God!" Thomas exclaimed.

Then Jesus told him, "You believe because you have seen me. Blessed are those who haven't seen me and believe anyway."

John 20:26-29

REAL Xpressions

Where Is God?

I can remember when I first met Christ. I was 16, and it was just like being in love. I know that sounds cheesy, but seriously, my heart would race whenever I would read the Bible. I would take long walks and pray for hours. And it was like Jesus was walking right by my side. Or I'd play a worship CD in my room and sing and sing and sing. And after awhile it was like I could *really* sense his presence.

Not anymore. Not for at least six months. Now it's like God has pulled back. And at the same time, all those passionate feelings I used to have are gone. My Christian life is total work now. A friend told me this is a normal thing. Maybe so, but it's still a drag. Especially given some of the problems that have popped up in my life.

I have been struggling with my relationship with my boss at work. He *never* leaves me alone. It gives me the creeps. Every time I get called in his office, I make sure the door is wide open and that I have an escape route at hand. I don't know what to do, and my friends in my Bible study have been no help. They think I'm imagining it and that he's really trying to be friendly, like a father figure to me. All I know is that my father never looked at me that way.

Then, there's my ministry at church. I work with the four-year-olds, and there's no joy. I used to really love helping in the class, but now it's just a chore. I dread Sunday mornings because I know I have to spend 60 long minutes with those brats.

I know my attitude is bad. I know I need to pray about it. I know I need to trust. But I just feel that God is nowhere near and that my prayers are just bouncing off the walls.

Samantha

REAL QUESTION

Following the death of his wife, in his classic book *A Grief Observed,* author C. S. Lewis asks: "Meanwhile, where is God? . . . [Go] to him when your need is desperate, when all other help is vain, and what do you find? A door slammed in your face, and the sound of bolting and double-bolting on the inside. After that, silence. You may as well turn away."

That sounds harsh, unless you've ever been through a period of darkness, a time of suffering. Those familiar with pain know the drill. They ask the same question asked by believers through the ages, the question, "Where is God when it hurts?"

REAL answer

People accuse the Bible of being lots of things, but one charge they can't legitimately make is that the Bible is "phony." It's not. You want reality? You want honesty that goes all the way to the bone? Read the psalms.

As you do, notice that David (together with the other psalmists) frequently asked, in so many words, the very same question above: *Where are you, God?* Take a look at the following:

- Psalm 10:1 "O LORD, why do you stand so far away? Why do you hide when I need you the most?"
- Psalm 22:1 "My God, my God! Why have you forsaken me? Why do you remain so distant? Why do you ignore my cries for help?"
- Psalm 13:1 "O LORD, how long will you forget me? Forever? How long will you look the other way?"
- Psalm 27:9 "Do not hide yourself from me. Do not reject your servant in anger. You have always been my helper. Don't leave me now; don't abandon me, O God of my salvation!"
- Psalm 88:14 "O LORD, why do you reject me? Why do you turn your face away from me?"

Do you get the picture? Feeling abandoned by God, feeling like God isn't near and doesn't hear is a very common experience, even by faithful servants like King David! Even Jesus, on the cross, felt this same kind of lonely despair (Matthew 27:46). If that's where you are, be encouraged by the truth that many others, including Christ, know how you feel.

The common experience of many Christians is that the first months (even years) of faith are filled with warm, tingly feelings. Most believers, however, report that the day eventually comes when the bottom drops out. The heart and soul seems to go dry. Intimacy with God seems to disappear. Suddenly, intense spiritual longings and vivid emotional experiences seem to be a thing of the past. Why? What's up?

In those times, God is forcing us to walk by faith and not by sight. The spiritual life would be a piece of cake if we could *always* sense God's presence in a tangible way. That wouldn't require faith at all. It's when we cry out and reach out to God when we *can't* sense him that our relationship with him deepens and grows. The effect is this agonizing search is deeper and longer lasting.

Realize that Jesus has promised to never actually leave you (Matthew 28:20) or forsake you (Hebrews 13:5). He's with you through thick and thin. But understand he may go into hiding, so to speak, to force you to grow up in your faith. Will you keep trusting Jesus when you've stopped "sensing" him? *That* is the real measure of maturity.

REAL YOU

A time in my life (maybe
even now) when God
seemed distant was
_____. I got through that
situation by . . .

_____

_____

_____

_____

_____

_____

_____

_____

_____

_____

_____

_____

_____

_____

_____

_____

_____

_____

_____

Some things I would say to a new Christian who was discouraged because God seemed distant are:

_____

_____

_____

_____

_____

_____

_____

_____

_____

_____

_____

_____

_____

Xalted

Counselor

Isaiah prophesied that the coming Messiah would be a Wonderful Counselor (Isaiah 9:6). Christ is indeed that. He guides us through the rough times of life, showing us where to go, and what to do. If you are struggling right now and feel that you are alone, ask for the Counselor to come alongside you, to walk with you through the times of testing.

Is it just the last few generations or have people *always* been so hungry for love? Think about it, the majority of songs and most movies depict this universal longing to know and be known, to accept and be accepted.

GOD'S LOVE—JESUS' IDENTITY AND WORK

On closer inspection, it's clear there is much confusion on the subject, not to mention millions of people devastated by failed attempts at love (strange that something so wonderful can cause so much pain).

The next seven devotions have to do with various aspects of love. They remind us that Jesus is the love of God in the flesh. He came to show us how love was meant to be expressed. When we move toward him and open ourselves up to him, we are transformed. And from that moment on, we become partners in an amazing cosmic romance.

I discover the Jesus Answer when I trust in the eyewitness reports about Jesus found in the Bible.

So the Word became human and lived here on earth among us. He was full of unfailing love and faithfulness. And we have seen his glory, the glory of the only Son of the Father.

John 1:14

REAL Xpressions

Searching for the Real Jesus

"Jesus? C'mon, Ryan, don't give me that 'Jesus' stuff! You might as well bring up the Easter bunny or the tooth fairy."

"What? Are you saying Jesus never existed?" My friend Craig has always been what you might say on the skeptical side of what he calls my "religion deal." But I can't help it. When he starts on his kick, I've got to answer. Here's how it usually goes:

"Maybe. Why is that statement any less valid than you saying he *did* exist?"

"Because of all the evidence. Good grief, Craig! Open your eyes, dude! Of course he existed! There's way more proof for Christ than there is for a lot of other stuff from ancient history!"

"Oh like what? Like the Shroud of Turin, the supposed 'actual burial cloth of Christ'?"

"Not necessarily. I don't know whether that's for real or not. We may never know. But it doesn't really matter. There are documents and stuff. Manuscripts."

"Oh, like the Bible, I guess."

"Yeah, exactly. Like 'the Bible.'"

"Well, I tell you what, Ryan. You can say whatever you want. But after watching that show on cable last night, I'm not sure the Bible is all that reliable. And I have *serious* doubts about whether Jesus even existed."

"Oh, so what? People just created Jesus out of thin air. We imagined him, and then made up all these stories, and now the billion or more people around the world who believe in Jesus are just idiots! Is that it?"

"Hey, *you* said that, Ryan. Not me."

And that's where we usually leave it. Until the next time. Some day . . .

Ryan

REAL QUESTION

Ever hear a debate like the one Craig and Ryan are having? Ever been in the middle of such a discussion?

It's not just an argument over semantics or a silly way to kill time while waiting for the instructor to show up. What they're grappling over is a pretty important issue. (Maybe that explains why things got a little heated between the two classmates.) At stake is the whole Christian faith.

How *do* we know Jesus existed?

REAL ANSWER

By any objective, historical standard, the Bible has to be regarded as an impressive and reliable collection of documents. Not only were most of the individual books of Scripture written soon after the fact (important for recording historical events with accuracy), but the *quantity* of manuscript copies is huge, and the *quality* is stunning. Scholars who have compared the oldest existing biblical records to copies made centuries later find few discrepancies (and these happen to be only minor changes that do not significantly alter the meaning of the text). In other words, the ancient scribes who copied these sacred writings down through the centuries, took enormous pains to reproduce them with 100% precision.

But even if a skeptic dismisses the Bible, he or she still has to decide what to do with the handful of references to Jesus in secular historical works from the period. Why in the world would these smart, non-Christian writers depict a mythical figure as a real person of history? If they were wrong on this matter, why should we believe anything else they say? But if they were right, well then . . . (you get the point).

Here's what one of the Bible historians said:

"The one who existed from the beginning is the one we have heard and seen. We saw him with our own eyes and touched him with our own hands. He is Jesus Christ, the Word of life. This one who is life from God was shown to us, and we have seen him. And now we testify and announce to you that he is the one who is eternal life. He was with the Father, and then he was shown to us. We are telling you about what we ourselves have actually seen and heard, so that you may have fellowship with us. And our fellowship is with the Father and with his Son, Jesus Christ" (1 John 1:1-3).

John was an eyewitness to history, to the Incarnation, to the teachings and miracles—to the remarkable life of Christ. The apostle Paul is another key witness. And his story is, perhaps, even more extraordinary. A staunch opponent of the Christian faith, a fanatic bent on putting believers in Jesus to death, Paul abruptly became a hard-core, lifelong follower of Christ one day on the Damascus Road. What prompted this totally unexpected turnaround? According to him, nothing less than a face-to-face encounter with the risen Jesus.

People can say what they will and believe what they want. But in trying to turn the historical Jesus into a myth, they have to ignore mountains of compelling evidence.

If you are a believer in Christ, you do not have to hang your head when so-called "scholars" begin questioning the historicity of Jesus. The evidence is there. Our faith rests on solid historical data.

REAL YOU

The three biggest questions I have about Jesus Christ are:

_____

_____

_____

_____

_____

_____

_____

_____

_____

_____

[Note: If you want to find answers to your questions or strengthen your ability to defend your faith in front of skeptics, you might wish to read Lee Stroebel's award-winning books *The Case for Christ* and *The Case for Faith*, or the student versions of these two books.]

The next time I get in a discussion about my faith with an unbeliever, here are three key points I need to make:

_____

_____

_____

_____

_____

_____

_____

_____

_____

_____

_____

_____

Xalted

Word of God

When the Bible refers to
Jesus as the "Word of God" (see,
for example, Revelation 19:13) it
means he is a living explanation of God.
His whole life is a show-and-tell description
of the character of the Creator. At a specific point
in history, countless people had personal dialogues
with this living "Word." As a result, we can be certain of the reality of Jesus, and we can know the heavenly Father he came to reveal.

I discover the Jesus Answer when I understand what it meant for Jesus to die in my place on the cross.

"...for this is my blood, which seals the covenant between God and his people. It is poured out to forgive the sins of many."

Matthew 26:28

REAL XPRESSIONS

Strange Way to Save the World

My friends and I were up late last Friday night talking and channel surfing, and of course, as we got up into the bigger numbers, we started seeing all these TV preachers.

As a Christian, I'm used to that. I've gotten to where I can just kind of shake my head and keep clicking. I figure Christians are like any other family. You always have a few quirky, weird "relatives." I think a lot of these people, for all their goofiness, are truly sincere. They're just trying to serve God the best way they know how. It's not *my* way, but, hey, it takes all kinds I guess.

Anyway, my friends aren't quite so tolerant. We came across this one preacher, complete with the hair and the bad suit, and he was all worked up over "the blood of Christ." I mean, if he said that phrase once, he said it a thousand times. By the end he was wild-eyed and sweaty and he was jumping around like he'd just won the lottery.

Cameron hit the mute button. "*That's* what gets me!" she said, pointing at the screen.

"What?" I asked.

"The way Christians obsess over death and blood. It's like the whole Bible is just this big bloody book. All the sacrifices. Animals being killed left and right. And for what!? And then Jesus gets crucified. And then Christians get killed for believing in Jesus. It's just so weird . . . all of it. Where's the love in all that and the peace? Tell me, Marcy, what about all that, is supposed to make me want to believe in God?"

Everybody sat there staring at me. And honestly, I didn't know what to say.

Marcy

REAL QUESTION

Maybe you've heard the song, often performed around Christmastime, which tells the story of Jesus coming to earth as a babe and growing up to die on the cross. The chorus asks the haunting question, "Isn't that a strange way to save the world?"

When you think about it, it *is* rather bizarre. A baby, born in a stable, who spends his first 30 or so years out of the public eye, doing God only knows what? Then suddenly he bursts on the scene, teaching and doing miracles, only to be rejected by his own people and publicly executed?

Why would God set about rescuing the human race in such an odd way? What's the big deal about the cross? Why did Jesus have to die?

REAL answer

The place to start is with what the Bible calls "sin." The more you read, the more you realize that sin is not just making a mistake, or messing up or forgetting to think before we act. Sin is deliberate disobedience. Sin is a creature declaring his or her independence from the Creator. Sin is humanity saying to Deity, "I can do whatever I want—I don't have to do what you say, and I won't."

Such rebellion, such arrogance is shocking. It is like telling God to take a hike. And according to the Bible, we're all guilty of this (Romans 3:23), whether we shake our fist at God or just ignore him.

In his perfect wisdom and love, God determined that sin must dealt with. First, because it is an offense against a holy God, it must be punished (or God would be guilty of eternal injustice). The sentence decreed for this capital crime? Death. It makes sense that the consequence for rejecting the author of life would be separation from life—or spiritual death (Romans 6:23).

Second, because sin is a very real kind of spiritual cancer (wreaking havoc and grief in and upon humanity) it must be destroyed. But how? It seems that such a terrible radical disease would require a radical cure.

God's solution? The cross. Not just a senseless, barbaric execution, the death of Jesus was deliberately arranged in order to both satisfy God's justice and show his love. Since the penalty for sin was death, Jesus paid it. He willingly experienced the horror of spiritual separation from God so we wouldn't have to (Matthew 27:46). He acted as our substitute.

When you think about it, once you get past the sheer gruesomeness of so-called Good Friday, God's plan for saving the world is really quite brilliant. In requiring the payment of death for sin, God demonstrated his perfect justice. And in sending his own son to be our substitute, God displayed his infinite love. In raising Christ from the dead, God, in effect, put his stamp of approval on this whole salvation plan. Anyone who wants the benefits of Jesus' sacrifice—forgiveness, a fresh start, and a right relationship with God, eternal life—can have them. They are offered to all as a free gift and become yours the moment you accept them with humility, faith, and gratitude.

Because of "the blood," God gets glory, and we get eternal life. Call it whatever you want, but that sounds like a pretty good deal all around.

REAL YOU

When I read the crucifixion account from one of the Gospels (Matthew, Mark, Luke, or John), these things make the biggest impression on me:

_____

_____

_____

_____

_____

_____

_____

_____

_____

_____

_____

_____

Because of Jesus' death on the cross, three specific actions I can take today are:

_____

_____

_____

_____

_____

_____

_____

_____

_____

_____

_____

_____

_____

Χalted

Lamb

In the Old Testament, animals—
most commonly sheep—were sacri-
ficed in place of people to pay for sins
committed. When Christ came, he was called
"the Lamb of God who takes away the sin of the
world" (John 1:29; see also Revelation 7:9-10). His
death on the cross was the full and final sacrifice for sin.
It both satisfied God's perfect justice and demonstrated his perfect love for the world.

I discover the Jesus Answer when I thank God that he loved and chose me, a sinner, as his.

"And I, the Son of Man, feast and drink, and you say, 'He's a glutton and a drunkard, and a friend of the worst sort of sinners!' But wisdom is shown to be right by what results from it."

Matthew 11:19

REAL XPRESSIONS

Unworthy?

I looked around the room at the people gathered for this prayer time and here's what I saw:

Courtney, who's pretty enough to be modeling in New York or LA. But she is so *"not* impressed with herself." In fact, she is all about other people.

I see Matt, who's funny and friendly and always has a crowd of people hanging around him. I think he could announce a trip to the city landfill and probably get a busload of people to sign up.

There's Ying, who is an out-an-out genius—straight A's, plays like five instruments and speaks three languages.

Mallory's multitalented too. Caleb can play guitar and sing like nobody's business. And all these people are really serious about God. It's *not* just one more thing to do with them. Jesus is really the center of their lives and they try to use what they're good at for him.

Then . . . there's me. What have *I* got to offer? I'm not good-looking or especially smart, or athletic, or popular or talented. In fact, I'm not real *anything.* And spiritually? Ha. Who am I kidding? I blow it. Mess up. Make dumb, wrong choices all the time. I bet I haven't even read the Bible in a month. As a matter of fact, I'm not exactly sure where I left my Bible!

Each week it's a struggle to come to this group. Not because people don't accept me. They do. Everyone is super nice. But when I compare myself to everyone else here, I just feel like I don't fit. They've all got *lots* to offer God. Not me.

Spencer

REAL QUESTION

Insecurity strikes whenever we feel inadequate about something—looks, smarts, popularity, ability, or whatever. Insecurity is one of those things that confronts all people some of the time and some people all the time.

It's safe to say that Spencer is feeling inferior in just about every way possible. At his prayer meeting, he feels spiritually inadequate, as though everyone else has a head start. He feels unworthy. Bottom line, he's feeling like he needs to be a certain way in order for God to love him.

Can you relate? Have you ever had the thought that God loved (or at least liked) someone else more because of their greater talent or faith?

Is that how it works?

REAL ANSWER

No doubt about it—some people *do* seem especially blessed. Do a quick mental survey of the people in your life and you'll probably be tempted to think that God plays favorites. He doesn't (see Deuteronomy 10:17; Romans 2:11). Sure, God gives different people different gifts to use and different roles to play in his eternal plan (1 Corinthians 12). But nothing in the Bible suggests that some people are worth more to God than others.

Our world ranks and values people on the basis of superficial things like money, beauty, popularity, power, and so forth. God uses radically different criteria (1 Corinthians 1:26-27). Look, for example, at the people Jesus chose to be his followers. The twelve disciples were a motley bunch of rough, bickering, petty, mostly uneducated guys. They weren't in anybody's "Who's Who?" They were average and unspectacular, with questionable credentials and character. And when it came to grasping spiritual truth, they were not especially "quick." When we first meet them in the Gospels there is nothing about them to suggest that they will ever amount to anything. As we read about their bumbling ways and their shocking spiritual ignorance, we might ask, "Why didn't Jesus at least select a trained rabbi or two, and maybe even a popular politician?"

The answer is that God doesn't choose us and love us *because* we have certain qualities or gifts or *because* we do good things or don't do bad things. He doesn't prefer us more if we perform in an acceptable manner or when we get our act together. With Jesus, it's not love *because* or love *if*, or love *when*—it's love, period. He just does.

We don't deserve God's love. Our good qualities don't earn us his favor; our failures don't cause him to withdraw his affection. His love is a choice, an eternal decision to seek us, find us, bless us, help us, and change us for the better. All that is good he wants to give us. Mostly, he wants to give us himself.

So, if you're like Spencer, stop comparing. God doesn't want you to imitate anyone else. He made you unique and desires for you to play a special role in his plan for the world. It's a vital role only you can play. He's far more interested in what you can become than what you currently are.

REAL YOU

When I am feeling inse-
cure and that God loves
or likes other people
more, I will remember the
following:

_____

_____

_____

_____

_____

_____

_____

Some of the unique gifts, talents, attributes, and experiences God has given me are:

_____

_____

_____

_____

_____

_____

_____

_____

_____

_____

_____

_____

_____

_____

_____

_____

_____

_____

_____

_____

_____

_____

ΧALTED

Friend of Sinners

One of the most shocking things about Jesus is the way he was drawn to "sinners" and they to him (Matthew 11:19). Whereas many people today with messed-up lives won't go anywhere near a church or a Christian for fear of coming away feeling even worse about themselves, "unworthy" people in Jesus' day sought him out. The reason? He always treated people with acceptance, compassion, and grace. And that's the way he'll always treat you.

I discover the Jesus Answer when I celebrate a person's acceptance of Jesus as his or her Savior.

His father said to him, "Look, dear son, you and I are very close, and everything I have is yours. We had to celebrate this happy day. For your brother was dead and has come back to life! He was lost, but now he is found!"

Luke 15:31-32

REAL Xpressions

Party in Heaven?

I've been involved at church for as long as I can remember. You know the type, member of the choir (six years), member of the church basketball team (three years), yearly participant in Vacation Bible School (forever!) and now an active member of my youth group for four faithful years.

While the group doesn't have officers or designated student leaders, I have to confess, most students look up to me. Maybe because I'm always there; maybe because they think I've got something to offer them. (I *always* participate in class discussions.) It's like I'm the unofficial president of the group. Or to put it another way: for whatever reason, I've got a lot of influence.

Lately, however, everyone's been making a huge fuss about this new guy in the group. Mark is a senior at Hoffman High School and one of the funniest, craziest, and most popular guys around. He signed up for a recent youth group ski retreat (shock!) and actually came (bigger shock!). But most amazing of all is that during the weekend, Mark expressed a desire to become a follower of Christ.

That was a little over a month ago. As far as I could tell, Mark seems totally sincere. John, the youth pastor, has been spending a lot of time with this new Christian, meaning John *hasn't* been hanging out with me as much as he used to. And at youth meetings, people cluster around Mark like he's a rock star.

If I were to be totally honest, I would tell you I feel blown off and more than a little irritated. I haven't said anything to anybody about it, but if you really want to know how I feel, here it is: Here's this guy who has spent his whole high school career being a jerk, getting drunk, and sleeping around. Now he comes on one retreat, and people are acting like he's one of the twelve apostles! I'm not saying Mark's not sincere. I really hope he is. But I just think he ought to be treated like everybody else.

Maybe some people will say, "Aw, Seth, you're just jealous!" But it's not that. Not at all.

Seth

REAL QUESTION

What's going on here? You think Seth is just irritated because Mark has replaced him as the center of attention? Or does he have a legitimate beef? Is it right to put new Christians on a pedestal? Should we get so "jazzed up" when someone makes a decision for Christ?

What about *you?* Ever been in a situation like the one above? Either in Seth's shoes or Mark's? What was that like?

What would Jesus say if he physically showed up at youth meeting one night? What would he say to Mark? To Seth?

REAL ANSWER

We don't have to *wonder* what Jesus might say or do in such a situation. In Luke 15, he tells a story almost identical to the scenario above. The story is about a father and two very different sons. The older son is faithful, always doing what his dad says. The younger son is a rebel who runs away, basically so he can raise hell. In time, when this irresponsible young man comes home, not so much because he's sorry for what he's done, but mostly because he's run out of money, the father throws him a party instead of reprimanding him! The older son is incensed, even though his dad insists, "I've *always* loved you just as much and would have been glad to throw a party for you *any-time*."

Finishing his story Jesus basically said, "That's how it works with God. All heaven celebrates when a rebellious person—even a real jerk—comes back home."

Jesus' reaction shouldn't shock us. In many ways, we do the same thing. If your dad came home from work, and said, "Guess what? I worked hard today. I did a good job" you'd think, "Huh? Why are you telling me this? You think that's *news*—that you did your job?" But if your dad came home from the doctor's office shouting: "Guess what? You know that cancerous tumor I had in my lung? It's gone!"—you'd do cartwheels across the living room.

Salvation is the biggest and best news of all. It's the dead coming to life. It's the lost being found. It's getting a fresh start. It's being transformed from God's enemy into God's cherished child. That's why when a person encounters Christ and decides to believe in him and follow him, it is a *huge* deal. That's why heaven throws a party! And that's why *we* should get excited.

And yet this amazing love of God, this shocking willingness to forgive sin, often becomes "ho-hum" news to lots of Christians. Even in their own lives they're like, "Yeah, that's neat. Great. I'm forgiven." But the truth no longer surprises or stuns them. They act almost as though they had it coming. As though they deserved it.

Other people, however, never get over Christ's love. They sing about it in church and just bust out laughing or even dancing. Or while celebrating their salvation in communion, they come unglued, tears and grape juice getting all over their clothes. That's the kind of grateful people we need to strive to be.

When God includes new people in his family, it doesn't mean he cares for us less. He's got more than enough love for the whole world. A heavenly party happened when you put your faith in Christ. It happens every time a rebellious prodigal comes to his or her senses and returns home. It's our job to keep the party going in our own hearts.

REAL YOU

In the story of the
"prodigal son," the person
I most identify with is
_____ because ...

_____

_____

_____

_____

_____

_____

_____

If I could speak with someone like Seth, I would give him this advice . . .

_____

_____

_____

_____

_____

_____

_____

_____

_____

_____

Xalted

Savior

As long as a person views himself or herself as OK and not in need
of rescue, there is no thought given to
spiritual salvation. For those who recognize
the helplessness and hopelessness of sin, the
thought of Christ as "Savior" is precious (Luke 2:11).
Christ came, he said, for that very reason, to seek and
save the lost (Luke 19:10). And when he does that, he throws a
party.

I discover the Jesus Answer when I understand that hell is a choice made by people who reject God.

"Just as the weeds are separated out and burned, so it will be at the end of the world. I, the Son of Man, will send my angels, and they will remove from my Kingdom everything that causes sin and all who do evil, and they will throw them into the furnace and burn them. There will be weeping and gnashing of teeth."

Matthew 13:40-42

REAL Xpressions

Hell? Yes

A loud, showy street preacher has really ruffled some feathers near campus. I've been amazed at the reaction of my two best friends, one a believer and the other not. It's really got me thinking about what I believe, too.

Kevin, who I have known since high school, claims he doesn't believe in anything except "today" and "myself." Basically, he thinks that the preacher's a joke. But he is disturbed by what the guy has to say, particularly about hell. At lunch today, he starting going off about him, "He ought to be ashamed trying to scare people with all his talk about 'sin' and 'hell'. If there *is* a God, and if he doesn't need anyone or anything, why should he care what we do? Why the need to punish? That's the thing that gets me most about Christians. They say stuff like, 'God loves the world. He loves you *so* much. He wants to give you eternal life.' But then they say, 'If you screw up, he will fry you in hell for all eternity.' Huh? What is *that?* Don't they hear how schizophrenic that sounds? Like God is this big, vengeful, insecure Creator. And *that* message is supposed to make people want Christianity?"

Whoa. I had to sit there a minute. I mean, Kevin was *so* hostile. Then Barrett jumped in. I met Barrett at the campus Christian fellowship group, and we hit it off. But I was surprised when he said he was troubled by the message of the evangelist: "At some level, I *do* agree with the guy, but I don't like the way he's going about it. It's almost like he's *glad* some people are going to be apart from God forever. He sure doesn't come across as very loving. I guess the only good thing about that guy being here is that at least some of my friends are willing to talk about God. But, of course, the first thing they want to discuss is hell. They say things like, 'So, you're saying that according to the Bible, if I don't "accept Jesus," I'm going to hell?' Man! I'll be honest—that's a topic that freaks me out. I'm not sure what I think, and I'm really not sure what to say."

I have to agree with Barrett. How *does* a Christian even begin to answer such questions?

Jip

REAL QUESTION

To which of the guys above do you relate more easily—Kevin or Barrett?

The idea of hell does indeed sound mean and cruel to a lot of people with its mention of fire and torment for all eternity. Not only does it sound a bit excessive, but it also sounds at odds with Jesus' teachings of forgiveness and love.

What does the Bible say? Is there really such a place? Why would God send someone there? How should a Christian understand this belief and explain it to others?

REAL answer

According to the Bible, hell is a real place. It's an actual destination, not a just a spiritual image. Hell is described as a pit (Revelation 17:8; 20:3), a place of fiery torment (Luke 16:23-28), and even a prison (Revelation 20:7).

Jesus spoke matter-of-factly about hell in Matthew 25:31-46. He told his listeners that people had only two destinations: eternal punishment and eternal life. He also used terms like "the outer darkness" and asserted that "in that place there will be weeping and gnashing of teeth" (Matthew 25:30). People argue about whether these descriptions are meant to be taken literally, but at the very least, the picture painted is one of desolate loneliness, separation from God, for all eternity. To deny the existence of hell is to make Jesus either misinformed or, worse, a liar.

It's important to understand that hell is *not* a sentence given to unwilling, innocent creatures. As C. S. Lewis once observed, there are only two kinds of people in the end: those who say to God, "Thy will be done" and those to whom God says, "Your will be done." Does it make sense that people would want to spend 20, 50, or 80 years on this earth running from God and rejecting his involvement in their lives, and then suddenly upon death have an overwhelming desire to be in his presence forever? Obviously not. People who resent God's rule right now are not suddenly going to want him as their king when they die. In short, then, hell is a choice.

Those who exclude God from their lives here and now experience a mini-preview of hell. Death, whenever it comes, is simply the continuation of that God-less existence, only to an infinite and eternal degree.

God's presence makes heaven the perfect, wonderful place that it is. And God's absence makes hell the terrible place that it is. So the choice comes down to this: does a person want God or not? And in making that most important of all choices, human creatures need to understand this sobering truth: There is no heaven without God.

REAL YOU

After reading 1 Timothy 2:4 and 2 Peter 3:9, this is how I believe God feels about those who reject him:

_____

_____

_____

_____

_____

_____

_____

_____

_____

_____

_____

_____

This is how I would explain the idea of hell to a skeptical classmate or a fearful friend:

_____

_____

_____

_____

_____

_____

_____

_____

_____

_____

_____

_____

_____

_____

_____

Χαlteᴅ

Deliverer

To be delivered is to be rescued. You are in trouble, in danger, in peril, but a deliverer comes on the scene to pull you to safety just in the nick of time. Jesus Christ is the ultimate Deliverer (Romans 11:26), wanting to spare helpless and hopeless people from an eternity of loneliness and torment in a real place called hell.

I discover the Jesus Answer when I reject stereotypes and love as Jesus loves.

"I command you to love each other in the same way that I love you."
John 15:12

REAL XPRESSIONS

Preconceived Notions

I have a friend who says, "Stereotypes exist for a reason." I know it's not a very politically correct thing to say, but I always agreed with him. You know, I thought certain types of people had certain reputations because they earned them.

I never thought my attitude was that big of a deal until I realized just how much judging I did every day. Like, if I saw an Asian girl at school, I automatically assumed that she was smart. If I saw a football player, I automatically assumed that he was a player when it came to girls, too. If I saw a cheerleader, I automatically assumed that she was sleeping with at least a couple football players.

Something happened last week, though, that really shook me up. I was talking with a couple of my friends in the hall when a cheerleader walked by. I made some comment about her, and she heard me. But instead of having one of her football-playing boyfriends hurt me badly, like I thought she'd do, she broke down. She came over and asked me why I would say something like that about her when I didn't even know her. She had tears in her eyes and looked really hurt. I didn't think she'd care what I thought of her.

I felt like a total idiot. At first, I tried to pretend like I was joking. Then I just said, "I'm sorry, I'll never say anything like that again." And I meant it.

I can't believe that she was really hurt by what I thought of her. I wonder how many other people I've hurt like that without knowing it. Now I understand why the Bible says judging others is a bad thing to do.

Roger

Real question

Stereotyping requires a few steps: First you have to get all your labels together. In other words you mentally list all the possible categories into which a person can fit (these can be racial, socio-economic, academic, athletic, body-type, political preference, music preference, church affiliation, and so forth). If you're into labeling, the good news is that there are *tens of thousands* of categories at your disposal. Next you get to assign relative values to each group. Example: "Why would *anyone* ever choose country music over R&B?" Then comes the fun part of sorting everyone out (for example, "she's white; I'm black" or "he's in the band; we're not" or even "she's a stereotype; but not *me!*").

The jocks make fun of "band geeks." The Goths look with contempt at the preps. The eggheads or brainiacs (or whatever they're called where you live) can't relate to the nerds. So you end up with a bunch of groups who look at each other with suspicion and distrust.

What are some of the stereotypes lodged in your head? What difference does the love of Christ make (or should make) when it comes to this very common, very human, very destructive habit of stereotyping?

Real answer

For the clearest and most concise answer take a look at Jesus' encounter with the woman at the well (John 4).

People had umpteen reasons for thinking that Jesus should never have even spoken with this woman. First was the whole gender thing. In that culture and that era, the sexes didn't mix and mingle much, especially in public. Men *might* bark a command to a wife in such a setting, but speak kindly to a stranger? It didn't happen. More significant than that, Jesus was a Jew, and this woman was a despised Samaritan. The Jews looked at the Samaritans as inferior half-breeds—not a real helpful attitude for building positive relationships. Finally, Jesus was a respected rabbi, a "holy man of God." And this woman? Well, the kindest way to say it is that she was a woman with a history of immorality. She had been married five times and the man she was living with now was not her husband.

Notice the way that Jesus ignored all these human-made, artificial barriers. He looked beyond the surface to the deep needs of this woman's heart. She was blown away by such unprecedented acceptance and kindness. The end result? Not only she, but also the whole town, was transformed (see John 4:39).

What about you? Two specific questions:

- Have you ever really grasped the truth that Jesus loves you just like you are? He doesn't categorize or label you—except maybe to regard you as "one of my deeply loved creatures." He doesn't stereotype you and lump you into a big group. In his eyes, you're a unique masterpiece, in a class all by yourself.
- Contrary to the example of Jesus, do you label people and judge them using superficial criteria (clubs they're in, where they live, what they wear or drive, skin color, preference in hobbies)?

Those who claim to be followers of Christ must try to live by this directive: "I command you to love each other in the same way that I love you" (John 15:12).

REAL YOU

I am guilty of stereotyping the following people in the following ways:

_____

_____

_____

_____

_____

_____

_____

_____

_____

_____

_____

_____

_____

_____

_____

Because Jesus has loved and accepted me unconditionally, I want to treat others in the same way. Specifically, I will show the love of Christ to the people above by taking the following actions:

_____

_____

_____

_____

_____

_____

_____

_____

_____

_____

_____

Xalted

Advocate

It's not just that Jesus accepts us.
According to the New Testament
(see 1 John 2:1), he is also our defender.
That's the meaning of the title "advocate."
In saving us, Jesus acts almost like a defense
attorney, lovingly representing us in the face of the
just accusations of a holy God. How much more should
we be advocates for those who face unjust prejudice and hurtful
labeling?

I discover the Jesus Answer when I accept God's views on sex.

"Since they are no longer two but one, let no one separate them, for God has joined them together."

Matthew 19:6

REAL Xpressions

Unmentionable

My friends laugh at me because I won't talk about sex. They can make me blush in two seconds flat if they bring it up in front of me. They all just seem to say whatever pops into their heads, no matter how embarrassing or disgusting it is. Not me.

I always get uncomfortable as soon as sex is mentioned. Maybe it's because my parents never talked to me about it. Whatever the reason, when I hear people talk about how great sex is, I cringe. I don't know, it just seems like there's something wrong about two people—well, you know.

When I told my youth leader how I feel, I really expected her to agree with me. But she didn't. Instead, she gave me one of those modern Bible translations and asked me to read the Song of Songs in the Old Testament.

So I did, and I couldn't believe what was in there! The whole book is this couple describing how much they want each other. If you put a picture of a half-naked couple on the cover, you could probably sell it as a romance novel.

After I got over the shock of seeing something like that in the Bible, I started wondering why it's in there. It's not like God punished those two lovers in the Song of Songs for what they were talking about. In fact, it seems like he's holding them up as an example of true love.

Finally I had to admit to myself that sex isn't something to be ashamed or afraid of. My youth leader said that sex is a gift from God, and that when it's expressed in the way he intended—between a husband and a wife—it's one of life's great pleasures.

Charlotte

REAL QUESTION

It might be *unusual* in this day and age, but it's not *bad* for Charlotte to be a little uneasy with public discussions of sex. Our culture used to be a little more discreet. Not anymore. Now, it's in your face everywhere you turn. Even little kids who really aren't yet old enough to process the basic facts of life are routinely subjected to graphic comments and or vivid descriptions of topics like oral sex and homosexuality.

Sadly, sex in our culture has become something to do with just about anyone, just about anywhere, pretty much whenever you want. It's viewed basically as body parts coming together for a few moments of physical pleasure. It's one more thing to do—wash the car, take out the garbage, do your homework, engage in sex—no big deal. Sex is even used to sell auto parts, chewing gum, TV dinners, whatever.

On the contrary, sex, the way God intended it, is the wonderful, beautiful, intimate, special, sacred, mysterious joining—not just of bodies, but of hearts, souls, and lives. It's a magnificent celebration of true, committed love, not a quick demonstration of bedroom abilities.

What's right? Should we view sex as a common, everyday, no-big-deal thing? Just a fun, physical act? Or is it more? And should it be reserved only for marriage?

REAL answer

The New Testament has no chapters that record Jesus teaching explicitly on the subject of sex, but in a real sense, the whole Bible is the written word of Christ, the one called the living Word. And the Bible says plenty about the topic.

First, there seems to be a twofold purpose for sex. Number one, to perpetuate the human species. After the flood, God spoke these words to Noah and his sons: "Now you must have many children and repopulate the earth. Yes, multiply and fill the earth!" (Genesis 9:7) How about *that* for a fun command? And the number two reason for sex: to celebrate the pleasures of marital love. Charlotte was blown away when she understood that, contrary to popular belief, the Bible is not prudish when it comes to sex. The Song of Songs shows that within the context of marriage, sex is intended to model on a physical level, the couple's spiritual and emotional commitment, love, and intimacy. And God must have intended for sex to be and feel amazing! (Why else would he have made it to be so pleasurable?)

Second, God has drawn clear boundaries for sex to keep it from being abused and misused and to protect us. Sex is to be reserved for marriage only, between a man and a woman (see Genesis 2:24; Leviticus 18:22; 1 Corinthians 6:18; Ephesians 5:3). Think about it—if people obeyed God's plan, no one would ever have to fear being an unwed mother or father, contracting an STD, or dragging a truckload of sexual guilt into a marriage.

God's rules on sex aren't meant to keep us from something good, but to keep us from something bad. He's not trying to deny us sexual pleasure; on the contrary, he wants us to experience the best sex. The Lord's prohibitions on sex are not to punish us, but to protect us and provide for us the best sex life imaginable.

If Jesus showed up in your bedroom right now (or wherever you happen to be), he might say something like this: "Truly, truly, I say to you: Sex *is* great and it *is* worth the wait. Accept it as one of my great gifts, but don't spoil it by opening it and using it before the time is right."

And one last reminder: No lovestruck couple that waited until marriage for sex was ever sad they did. But plenty of people who ignored God's sexual boundaries desperately wish they could turn back the clock.

REAL YOU

Because there is a world of difference between sex and love, I need to make the following changes in my attitudes and actions:

_____

_____

_____

_____

_____

_____

_____

_____

_____

_____

_____

_____

_____

Some practical and personal guidelines I'd like to follow in the area of sex and dating are:

_____

_____

_____

_____

_____

_____

_____

_____

_____

_____

_____

_____

_____

Xalted

Author of Life

An author creates a whole world. He or she gets to design characters and scenes and control a story to a desired conclusion. The Bible calls Christ the "author of Life" (Acts 3:15). This means that the world (and the way it works) is his idea. He knows what's best. He sets the ground rules. When it comes to topics like sex, we ought to pay careful attention to what he says.

A few years ago, U2's lead singer Bono was the voice for an entire generation when he wailed, "I still haven't found what I'm looking for." Which raises the question, exactly what *are* people looking for?

GOD'S TRUSTWORTHINESS AND TRUTH

We could list a million and one answers (we won't—aren't you glad?), but beneath them all is a desire for meaning and purpose. People want something stable and satisfying upon which to build their lives. (Don't you?) They want to know who or what they can trust. Or, put another way, in a world with so many options, they want to know what's right and best.

Christians believe the answers to these questions are found in Christ. But even then we sometimes wonder, *When life doesn't always turn out the way I hoped, how do I keep holding on to Jesus?*

That's what these next eight devotions are all about.

I discover the Jesus Answer when I search for truth in God's Word.

"Make them pure and holy by teaching them your words of truth."
John 17:17

REAL Xpressions

The Quest for Truth

It all started in Mrs. Blaine's class. We had a guest speaker from the local university—some anthropology professor who was talking about human cultures and governments.

Midway through his lecture, he kind of joked that some cultures promote the idea that you should "love your neighbor" while other more primitive cultures believe in *killing* their neighbors (and maybe even eating them). And somewhere in there, he made a statement about how truth is a relative thing, an abstract concept that can vary from culture to culture.

Well, a couple of strong Christians in the class took issue with that idea, and they started arguing about the Bible being true. This got several other people riled up. They started arguing that it was arrogant for any one group to act like its way was the best or only way. Finally, this girl name Chloe (who's really smart, but also kind of out there) went off on this big, long spiel about every culture having to come up with its own rules and ideas—whatever works for them. And that the same thing needs to happen even on the personal level. She babbled on for a while, but just before the class was over, she said something like, "So, you Christians can bang on the Bible, but in the end that's just your opinion, and if that works for you, great! But everyone else has to find his or her own truth. And we have to be willing to let the truth change over time and take us in new, different directions. Truth isn't some stale, constant thing. It's always evolving."

I think Chloe would have gone on another hour or so, but the bell rang, and so the argument spilled over into the lunch hour. What bugs me most is the way most of the class just sat there nodding like, "Wow. This is so deep!" *Sheesh*, I kept thinking, *Can't they see that what the professor and Chloe are saying is nuts!?* But I couldn't seem to figure out how to say that in a way that made sense.

Tom

REAL QUESTION

Ideas like those upheld by Chloe and the anthropology professor above are wildly popular today. The prevailing thinking in our culture seems to be that truth is *not* an objective reality that transcends all of life. Truth is viewed as a matter of one's own opinion. In a post-modern world we get to make up our own rules. Truth is within each one of us. To a great degree, we determine what is true. And so life is not about adjusting our lives to comply with some fixed, eternal reality; it's about creating our own reality and bending our rules to fit with our own desires.

In such a system, nothing is always right or always wrong. Everything "depends." Truth is whatever we decide it is. It's this kind of wishy-washy, "whatever" thinking that gives us laws, for instance, that say an abortionist can't be charged with a crime if he takes the life of an unborn child in his office, but if while driving home that evening he accidentally runs over the pregnant woman, killing her and her unborn child, he can be charged with two counts of vehicular homicide.

Is there such a thing as "absolute truth?" If there is, what is it? Are some things absolutely true (even if no one agrees with them), or is truth just whatever we say it is?

REAL answer

This is not just an academic question. The issue of truth is fundamental and essential. At stake are our culture, our law, and our future. Without a universal standard of right and wrong, anything goes. If there is no truth in the full and final sense, then Hitler wasn't the evil guy everyone makes him out to be. (After all he was only doing what he thought was right. And, hey, his own people were mostly behind him!) Without a final, ultimate standard, without objective truth that transcends human culture and individual preference, words and rules lose all meaning, and civilization degenerates into a chaotic mess where people are a law unto themselves.

It's interesting that Jesus spoke often and unashamedly of "truth." In John 8:32, he said, "And you will know the truth, and the truth will set you free." In John 14:6, he made the startling claim, "I am the way, the truth, and the life. No one can come to the Father except through me." Notice that Jesus did not claim to be "a" truth or "one of many truths." He said bluntly that he was "the" truth. By any estimation, that's a narrow and exclusive statement. It does not fit with the popular notion that any and every belief is equally valid. This is contrary to what you might hear on the news or in school.

The implication of Jesus' statements is that some things are *not* true. So where do we find this absolute truth for living? In John 17:17, Jesus claims that the Word of God is the ultimate reality.

He also promised to give his followers a personal tutor to help us make sense of the absolute truth of the Word of God, "When the Spirit of truth comes, he will guide you into all truth" (John 16:13).

REAL YOU

Some of the sources of "truth" that my friends and classmates lean upon for guidance are:

_____

_____

_____

_____

_____

_____

Because God's Word is the only sure and unchanging reality, I want to:

_____

_____

_____

_____

_____

_____

_____

_____

_____

_____

_____

Xalted

Truth

If something is true, it means it is trustworthy and dependable. A "true blue" friend will stick with you to the bitter end. A "tried and true" solution is a solution that always works. Jesus is the ultimate Truth (John 14:6). He will never mislead us. He will never let us down. We can trust him in every situation.

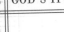

I discover the Jesus Answer when I live according to God's unchanging truth.

"Heaven and earth will disappear, but my words will remain forever."
Mark 13:31

REAL XPRESSIONS

Beauty Is Skin Deep

Billboards start advertising for swimsuits in the middle of winter, when I'm still wearing wool sweaters and boots. That's when I start stressing. It's that time again. As soon as the first sunny spring day arrives, my friends grab their bikinis and spend hours absorbing the rays. With sunglasses, beach towels, tanning oil, and water bottles in hand, they line their perfect bodies in a row on the beach. Their hair gets even blonder. Their tan lines become more defined, and every now and then, they even go in the water.

Every year at this time, I feel a slight panic. I don't have the perfect body—not even close. I know I'm flabbier than everyone else. Plus I'm fair-skinned and just don't tan. This year will be just like last year: unlike most of my friends, I'm not going to catch the eye of most guys within a two-mile radius. Realistically, I may not turn even a single head. It's hard to deal with this stuff, but it hurts even worse to try to become something I'll never be able to be.

I know the answer in my head. I've always known. It goes against everything in the movies, sitcoms, music videos, magazines, the popular crowd at school, and pop culture in general. The message of the Bible completely contradicts all those messages that bombard me every day. "Charm is deceptive, and beauty does not last; but a woman who fears the Lord will be greatly praised" (Proverbs 31:30). Jesus views things differently. He sees past my appearance to my heart, to what really counts. And all Christians are called to do the same.

Do verses like that make the swimsuit season any easier? A little bit. I guess sometimes they do. Although I still have days when I look in the mirror and get bummed out. When that happens I have to constantly remind myself what true, lasting beauty is and what it's not. I'm old enough to know that if I start thinking I need to have "the perfect body," I'll be a basket case. It's only when I manage to focus on God's message that I feel free.

Nora

REAL QUESTION

In our culture, magazine models are considered the ultimate standard for feminine beauty. Never mind if the cover girl is selfish, shallow, and conceited, for beauty has nothing to do with character. Beauty is all about great skin, gorgeous hair and eyes, a flawless figure, and pearly white teeth.

Or is it?

Beneath Nora's struggle is the deeper and more fundamental issue of what's really true. Who or what are we going to listen to as we develop convictions, establish values, and make decisions? Are we going to take our cues from friends and culture, or are we going to base our lives on biblical truth? It comes down to that basic choice: the multiple, mixed messages of the world or the consistent message of the Word of God.

Which is it going to be? Where will you get your values?

REAL ANSWER

If we look to our culture to tell us what's true, we will never find stability. What's "in" or "acceptable" today is "out" and "unacceptable" tomorrow. Look, for example, at how perceptions of beauty have changed in just a few years. A very curvy Marilyn Monroe was the "it" girl of the 50s and early 60s. By today's almost anorexic standards, poor Marilyn would be regarded as a cow! And it's not just ideas about beauty that change. Moral values also vary from culture to culture and from era to era.

We have a choice. We can try to live up to the fickle standards of a restless, constantly changing culture. Or we can make the life-changing decision to base our lives on the unchanging truth of God's Word. What a comfort! God's truth never changes. It is timeless. It is never out-of-date. Like an eternal rock it stands. It is applicable to all people of all nations for all times.

Consider the wise counsel of Jesus. Rather than obsessing over trivial issues of life, Jesus calls us to focus on more enduring issues. Listen:

"So I tell you, don't worry about everyday life—whether you have enough food, drink, and clothes. Doesn't life consist of more than food and clothing? Look at the birds. They don't need to plant or harvest or put food in barns because your heavenly Father feeds them. And you are far more valuable to him than they are. Can all your worries add a single moment to your life? Of course not.

"And why worry about your clothes? Look at the lilies and how they grow. They don't work or make their clothing, yet Solomon in all his glory was not dressed as beautifully as they are. And if God cares so wonderfully for flowers that are here today and gone tomorrow, won't he more surely care for you? You have so little faith!

"So don't worry about having enough food or drink or clothing. Why be like the pagans who are so deeply concerned about these things? Your heavenly Father already knows all your needs, and he will give you all you need from day to day if you live for him and make the Kingdom of God your primary concern."

Matthew 6:25-33

This is exactly what Nora is trying to do: focus on God and his kingdom. She's learning that it's not wrong to wear a bathing suit and work on a tan; neither is it right to obsess over it. Only a preoccupation with God's truth can keep us from going crazy!

REAL YOU

I find it difficult to keep God's truth at the forefront of my mind because I am bombarded daily by hundreds of wrong or conflicting messages from my culture. My biggest struggles lately are in these areas:

_____

_____

_____

_____

_____

Some Christian friends who can help me get a better handle on God's truth are:

_____

_____

_____

_____

_____

XALTED

Bridegroom

The ultimate groom in a wedding would be caring and kind, unselfish and eager to protect his bride. This is an apt description of Jesus Christ (Matthew 9:15). He wants what is best for us. He loves us and longs to see us set free from the curse of trying to live up to the constantly-changing standards of a misguided culture. He looks at us and sees nothing but beauty.

I discover the Jesus Answer when I commit myself to reading and learning God's Word.

"Anyone who listens to my teaching and obeys me is wise, like a person who builds a house on solid rock. Though the rain comes in torrents and the floodwaters rise and the winds beat against that house, it won't collapse, because it is built on rock."

Matthew 7:24-25

REAL Xpressions

Handling the Truth

The guest speaker is making the point that the Bible is the roadmap of the Christian faith, yet a huge percentage of self-proclaimed Christians haven't even read it completely. "If we really believe this book is God's Word, why don't we read it? Why do we treat it like a good luck charm—just a good thing to have around the house? When is it going to kick in that God has spoken to us, and given us a guide for life?"

Sure he makes sense. And he's right. If I'm a Christian, well, I should be reading God's Word and living by it. Great. Easy to say, but incredibly hard to do.

I know I'm supposed to get into the Word, but I don't have a clue how to do that. I bet I've started trying to read through the Bible five times. I always start strong. I get into Genesis and most of Exodus—no problem. It's really interesting stuff. But then I get to the end of Exodus where they start building the tabernacle, and then into Leviticus with all those long chapters about the sacrifices. And it's the same thing over and over in every chapter. I can't focus, so I just lose interest. Once I made it to Numbers, but then it was like, "And this tribe has this many people, and that tribe has this many . . ." Do I *believe* it's important to read the Bible? Absolutely. Do I know *how* to do that? No way.

I've even tried getting into a Bible study that meets right before school. I thought it would be a great way to get into the Word, but I wasn't counting on the early mornings! It's hard to get up at 5:30, grab my Bible, and then focus! I mean, this is difficult stuff to take in when my brain is only half awake.

There's got to be an easier way. It shouldn't be this hard.

Dennis

REAL QUESTION

In the last few pages, we said that absolute Truth *does* exist in this world and that we can find it in the pages of the written Word of God. Ah, but that raises the question: How do you take your sometimes hard-to-understand Bible and make sense of it?

Can you relate to Dennis's honest admissions? Why or why not?

Put a check mark by all the statements in the following list that accurately explain how you feel about the Bible:

☐ "I'm motivated to read it"

☐ "I don't see how it is relevant to my life"

☐ "I don't know where to begin"

☐ "It just doesn't grab me"

☐ "I'm in the Word pretty much every day"

☐ "I rarely pick up and read my Bible"

☐ "I know how to study the Word and apply it to my life"

☐ "I don't know Genesis from Jeremiah"

☐ "I get intimidated by the Bible"

☐ "I feel lost when I try to read the Bible"

☐ "I get lots of comfort from the Bible"

☐ "I don't even know where my Bible is"

REAL answer

The Bible is broken down into two main sections: the Old and New Testaments. The first four books of the New Testament are called the Gospels. These books, written by Matthew, Mark, Luke, and John, are four separate biographies of Christ. Not only are these a great place to start reading the Bible, but in these pages you'll notice something cool about Christ: He was the absolute master communicator.

Jesus was all about trying to help people understand God's truth. He wanted people to see it, grasp it, and live it out. And to make that happen he used all kinds of ingenious and creative teaching methods. He told stories. He asked questions. He used object lessons. He quoted extensively from the Old Testament (the New Testament hadn't even been written at the time Jesus was on earth). His goal? He wanted people to understand who God is and what it means to have a relationship with him. From this we can rightly conclude that Jesus wants today's Christians to understand and obey God's truth too.

How can we do this? Here are a few helpful tips:

Get a Bible translation you can understand. The King James Bible is known for its poetic beauty, but it was written in the language of a whole different culture. Some older Christians don't like to admit it, but the truth is Jesus did *not* speak in Elizabethan English. Try a newer, more modern version, like the New Living Translation (NLT).

Get a study Bible. Many study Bibles contain lots of helpful notes and features that explain hard-to-understand words and verses, aimed specifically for teens and young adults. Having the right study Bible is like having a Bible professor sitting with you while you read.

Listen to solid preaching and teaching. Take good notes when your pastor speaks. And, if possible, attend a "Walk Thru the Bible" seminar. Created by Bruce Wilkinson, author of the best-selling *Prayer of Jabez,* this interactive workshop is an ingenious and fun way to grasp the overall message of God's Word in just a few hours. More than a thousand of these seminars are held each year, all over the world.

Make it your goal to read through the Bible. No matter how you slice it, it *is* kind of strange when Christians talk about the Bible being God's

perfect Word, his revelation, his love letter to the world, his plan for living, and then in the next breath, admit that they've never even read the
whole thing. Commit to do this over the next year with a couple of
friends so you can encourage each other through the hard, dry chapters.
Find a one-year reading plan and stick to it—even if it takes more than
a year!

Real You

Some words or phrases I
would use to describe how I
feel about the Bible and about
my current understanding of it are:

_____

_____

_____

_____

_____

_____

Some specific changes I want to make in my Bible reading and study
habits are:

_____

_____

_____

_____

_____

_____

_____

_____

_____

Xalted

Lawgiver

God didn't *have* to communicate with humankind, but he did. He chose to reveal himself through creation, through his written Word, and through Jesus, the living Word. One title for Christ is "lawgiver" (Isaiah 33:22), which speaks of his gracious willingness to inform us of the wise, godly rules that make our lives more orderly and fulfilling. How well do you know Jesus' laws and commands? To know what he expects from you, read his words—then obey.

I discover the Jesus Answer when I make choices according to God's truth rather than my feelings.

"He is the Holy Spirit, who leads into all truth. The world at large cannot receive him, because it isn't looking for him and doesn't recognize him. But you do, because he lives with you now and later will be in you."

John 14:17

REAL XPRESSIONS

Feelings!

I always thought kids who went to Christian schools were different— you know, more conservative and more spiritual than the rest of us public school kids. So when Phillip invited me to his house to work on signs for our youth group fundraiser, I was a little nervous. Even though we joke around a lot in youth group, I wasn't sure about how I should act around him or what I should talk about.

Man, was *I* in for a shock!

His parents were on their way out the door when I got there. And as soon as they were gone, he said, "Hey, man, you want to look at some skin mags?"

I thought he was joking, so I played along. I said, "Yeah, sure, let me see Miss December." He went upstairs for a minute, and I thought he was getting poster board and markers and stuff like that. But then he came down, threw this magazine on the table right in front of me, and said, "I don't have the December issue, but check out the centerfold in that one."

He was serious!

I'm not going to lie to you—I wanted to look at it. I mean, give me a break, I'm a guy. I have the same kind of urges that everyone else does.

But I also know that Jesus knew what he was talking about when he said, "Don't even let lust get started in your brain." The problem is that once you get certain kinds of pictures in your head, it's hard to get them out. I know—it's happened to me before.

But it didn't happen this time because I told Phillip, "Thanks, but no thanks."

Bobby

REAL QUESTION

Bobby's dilemma raises an issue that Christians have to deal with everyday. Not simply the problem of lust. Not even the broader issue of temptation in general. Underneath all that is the more fundamental question of truth versus feelings. In the everyday moments of the real world, are we going to govern our lives according to God's truth or human hormones?

Our culture constantly feeds us the hedonistic philosophy of "eat, drink, and be merry." Beer commercials capture this mindset well. The way they depict it, life is all about good-looking people having good times and looking for sexual pleasure. We hear stories about ancient Rome, but its excesses were mostly limited to the rich and powerful. In our time, almost *everyone* has access to the Internet, to pornography, to easy credit, and to entertainment.

So for the Christian, the issue is not so much, "What's right?" (Usually we know.) It's more the question of "How in the world do I *do* right when everyone *outside* me and almost everything *inside* me is urging me to ignore what God has said is true?"

REAL ANSWER

Many believe that freedom means doing whatever you want. But talk to the 17-year-old who spends three or four exciting, but highly frustrating, hours a night drooling over pornography. Listen to the college sophomore who has run up over $10,000 in credit card debt. This kind of unrestrained living advertises itself as liberty; in truth, it is the most bitter form of slavery. Thanks to this version of "freedom" we have a society rampant with divorce, depression, and sexual disease.

Jesus spoke of a different path to happiness:

> "God blesses those who realize their need for him, for the Kingdom of Heaven is given to them.
>
> God blesses those who mourn, for they will be comforted.
>
> God blesses those who are gentle and lowly, for the whole earth will belong to them.
>
> God blesses those who are hungry and thirsty for justice, for they will receive it in full.
>
> God blesses those who are merciful, for they will be shown mercy.
>
> God blesses those whose hearts are pure, for they will see God.
>
> God blesses those who work for peace, for they will be called the children of God.
>
> God blesses those who are persecuted because they live for God, for the Kingdom of Heaven is theirs.
>
> God blesses you when you are mocked and persecuted and lied about because you are my followers. Be happy about it! Be very glad! For a great reward awaits you in heaven. And remember, the ancient prophets were persecuted, too."
>
> Matthew 5:3-12

What is he saying? That the world has it all wrong. Blessing isn't found in giving in to our sinful desires. Real freedom (in the biblical sense of the term) means the supernatural power to overcome sinful impulses, urges, and whims, and to live with self-control to the glory of God. Where does the power come from? From the Holy Spirit of God who moves into our lives when we first put our faith in Christ (Romans 8:9).

Christians do *not* live impulsively. We do not give in to every urge. We live purposefully and with discipline. We live thoughtfully and with discernment. We consider all possible consequences before we make choices.

As you make your way through days filled with temptation, as you wrestle with old desires that don't conform to God's truth, you can call upon God to help you. He is trustworthy, always eager to help his children live, not according to their raging hormones, but according to what is true.

REAL YOU

The places in my life where I struggle most with living by "how I feel" versus living by "what God's Word says" are:

_____

_____

_____

_____

_____

_____

_____

_____

_____

_____

_____

_____

_____

_____

_____

_____

_____

My "response plan" for next time I face serious temptation will be as follows:

_____

_____

_____

_____

_____

_____

_____

_____

_____

_____

_____

_____

Xalted

Master

The title "master" is difficult for 21st-century believers to grasp. It means "lord" and refers to one who calls all the shots, has all authority, and must be obeyed. Jesus Christ is every Christian's Master (Colossians 3:24). We do not have the right to debate over whether or not we will obey him. When he speaks, we must swing immediately into action, knowing that his commands are always good and right. Let Jesus be the "Master" of your life rather than your feelings.

I discover the Jesus Answer when I accept Jesus' view on tolerance, to love the sinner and not the sin.

"Teacher," they said to Jesus, "this woman was caught in the very act of adultery. The law of Moses says to stone her. What do you say?"

They were trying to trap him into saying something they could use against him, but Jesus stooped down and wrote in the dust with his finger. They kept demanding an answer, so he stood up again and said, "All right, stone her. But let those who have never sinned throw the first stones!" Then he stooped down again and wrote in the dust.

When the accusers heard this, they slipped away one by one, beginning with the oldest, until only Jesus was left in the middle of the crowd with the woman. Then Jesus stood up again and said to her, "Where are your accusers? Didn't even one of them condemn you?"

"No, Lord," she said.

And Jesus said, "Neither do I. Go and sin no more."

John 8:4-11

REAL Xpressions

Tolerance and Truth

I'm sick and tired of the whole political correctness movement. Everybody's scared to death to make value judgments about anything. You can't question anybody's behavior. You certainly can't suggest that certain things might be wrong because then you get called *intolerant*—which to a lot of people is like the worst thing in the world.

Take homosexuality, for example. At some level if people choose to do that, hey, it's their business. But at the same time, I shouldn't be forced to act like I approve of something that goes totally against my beliefs. I understand the need to keep a few crazy people from physically harming gays, but keeping regular people from *thinking* homosexuality is wrong or *saying* they don't agree with the practice? That's *way* over the line. In my mind tolerance means you let people quietly live their lives. It shouldn't mean you have to agree with everything they're doing or that you can't voice your honest opinions.

At least that's what I think. But when I expressed those thoughts at youth group the other night, I couldn't believe the response I got! This one girl, Candace, really lit into me. She told me that if I call myself a Christian then I ought to act like one. Christianity is all about love and acceptance, she said, and *then* she accused me of being a self-appointed "sin police." Whoa! But that wasn't all. She said she knew plenty of gays and lesbians who really love God.

So what's the truth? Who's right? Who's wrong? Sometimes I don't even know what to believe.

Will

REAL QUESTION

What do you think about the expressions above? Not so much the heated topic of homosexuality, but the various views on tolerance? How does a Christian balance truth and tolerance?

Here's another question: Is there ever an appropriate time to be intolerant?

How do we know there's one truth?

REAL ANSWER

Tolerance used to mean that you could make moral judgments all day long so long as you treated people with dignity and kindness. You could have a heated debate and agree to disagree. You could even say, "I think that's just plain wrong." In our day, the concept of tolerance has been distorted. Will's comments above are pretty accurate. Now tolerance means that every opinion is equally valid. Now tolerance means you not only have to accept people but approve of everything they do. Is this what Jesus advocated?

Not at all. The classic example is the story of the woman caught in adultery. Jesus treated this humiliated woman with great respect, but at the end of the day, he also instructed her to leave her "life of sin" (John 8:11, NIV). In other words, her behavior was wrong. Improper. Unacceptable. Illegitimate. And dare we say it—even "sinful."

On numerous other occasions Jesus expressed *strong* disapproval of the conduct of assorted people. It's important to realize he never stopped loving those he corrected, but he took issue with their wrong behaviors. He's exhibit A of what it means to love the sinner, but hate the sin.

When you get right down to it, the modern version of tolerance is downright goofy. Nobody is 100% tolerant, and if we were, society as we know it would cease to exist. We live with intolerance every day (and like it!). Our government doesn't tolerate terrorists. Judges and juries don't tolerate criminal behavior. Society doesn't tolerate drunk drivers going the wrong way down a one-way street. Doctors don't tolerate dirty instruments or unsanitary conditions in the ER.

Fact is, intolerance is quite often a good thing. And moral intolerance is a holy thing. If we believe what the Bible says and what Jesus taught, we are forced to conclude that not all beliefs are true and not all behaviors are acceptable, much less good and desirable. If you believe in truth, then you must also believe in error. If some actions are good, then opposing actions are not good.

REAL YOU

Based on what I've learned about tolerance, my thinking needs to change in this way:

_____

_____

_____

_____

_____

_____

_____

_____

_____

_____

_____

_____

_____

_____

_____

Here's what I might say to a friend who believed as Candace believes:

_____

_____

_____

_____

_____

_____

_____

_____

_____

_____

_____

_____

_____

Xalted

True Vine

In the Old Testament, Israel was commonly called God's vine. Over the years, however, Israel (led by the Levites and priests) strayed from God's truth and started following lots of wrong religious ideas, like worshiping false idols. By calling himself the "true vine" (John 15:1), Jesus meant that his ways and words are always in accordance with God's truth. As we stay connected to the vine, we will follow his teachings and never fear going astray.

I discover the Jesus Answer when I stand by his truth no matter what the consequences.

"But even more blessed are all who hear the word of God and put it into practice."

Luke 11:28

REAL XPRESSIONS

To Tell the Truth

It's a big, messy deal. And no matter what I do, my life is about to get really complicated.

Last night four (cute and popular) guys stopped by my house. No argument there. We all stood in my driveway and visited for probably 15 minutes total. Three of them—including Mike, the driver—had open beers. I also noticed a number of other empties on the floorboard. One of the guys made a joke to the effect of "Oh, this is nothing. We're just getting started!"

They left shortly after that, and I have to confess, I didn't think much about it at the time. I went back in the house and did my nails. But now I'm seeing the entire situation in a different light. It turns out their boss at the convenience store discovered a couple cases of beer missing last night and called the police.

Now the police are at *my* door wanting to ask me a couple questions.

As I walked down the hall toward the living room, my heart and mind were racing. *What if they ask me what I saw? I have to tell the truth, right? But what will everyone think?* I ducked into the bathroom and stared in the mirror. *Oh, what am I supposed to do? It's not like they're a bunch of drunks. Mike and Presley go to my church, for crying out loud!* So that's great. Am I'm supposed to rat on my Christian friends?

Now, as I pace between the toilet and tub, a hundred thoughts race through my mind all at once. *Can't I just plead the fifth amendment ... or plead no contest or—whatever? Or why can't I just say, "I don't remember"? Because the truth is I don't even remember what kind of beer it was.*

Omigosh. I feel like I'm gonna throw up!

Whitney

REAL QUESTION

Wouldn't you *hate* to be in Whitney's shoes? What would you advise her to do? What do you think you'd do (honestly) in that same situation? If she spills the beans, what are the likely consequences?

In times like this, we struggle with living truthfully and we wonder about God's trustworthiness. If we do what is right, will he really come through for us?

REAL answer

The apostle Peter was right there front and center when Jesus taught the lesson we know as the "Sermon on the Mount" (some scholars actually think Christ gave this message on more than one occasion). But whether it was once or ten times, obviously the strange and powerful words of Jesus burned their way into Peter's heart and mind. We know this because years later Peter issued similar instructions to a group of Christians facing big trouble:

"If you want a happy life and good days, keep your tongue from speaking evil, and keep your lips from telling lies. Turn away from evil and do good. . . . The eyes of the Lord watch over those who do right, and his ears are open to their prayers. But the Lord turns his face against those who do evil. . . . But even if you suffer for doing what is right, God will reward you for it. So don't be afraid and don't worry. . . . Keep your conscience clear. Then if people speak evil against you, they will be ashamed when they see what a good life you live because you belong to Christ. Remember, it is better to suffer for doing good, if that is what God wants, than to suffer for doing wrong!" (1 Peter 3:10-12, 14, 16-17).

What can we conclude from all that? Well, the life and teachings of Jesus (which echo through Peter's words above) remind us that as Christians we are called to a radically different standard. We should not follow the pattern of this world (Romans 12:2), because this world is not our home. We are expected to live by different values, beliefs, attitudes, and actions. This shouldn't be different in an arrogant or unattractive way, but different in an appealing, almost spiritually seductive way, enticing people to want to know more about the God you know and serve, the God who has been so good to you and who impacts all aspects of your life.

Make no mistake, if Whitney tells the truth, she might very well suffer for it. But she won't be alone. The faithful people of God through the ages have always paid a price for living according to God's truth. The patriarchs, the prophets, the apostles, and even Jesus were misunderstood, criticized, and condemned. What makes us think we will be treated any better? But God will reward us later for our faithfulness now.

REAL YOU

Because integrity means standing for truth all the time (not just when it's easy) I will make the following commitments and adjustments to my behavior:

_____

_____

_____

_____

_____

_____

_____

_____

_____

_____

_____

_____

_____

_____

_____

_____

Some friends of mine who are getting grief for standing for truth and who need my prayers are:

_____

_____

_____

_____

_____

_____

_____

_____

_____

_____

_____

_____

_____

_____

Xalted

Guardian of Your Soul

What if you had a bodyguard
who was the biggest and baddest
dude around? Would you fear anything,
anyone, or going anywhere? According to
1 Peter 2:25, Jesus is the "guardian of your
soul"—a fancy phrase that means "spiritual bodyguard." Christians need not worry. We have ultimate,
ever-present protection.

I discover the Jesus Answer when I trust that he will comfort me during difficult times.

"Don't be troubled. You trust God, now trust in me."
John 14:1

REAL XPRESSIONS

Big Changes

Every five years. That's how often my dad rips my life apart.

Five years ago, he told me that he and Mom were getting a divorce and that she was moving out. And now, five years later, just when I'm starting to get over that, he drops another bomb.

He's getting married again.

I knew he'd been spending a lot of time with Margie, but I never thought things were that serious between them. Even when he told me that he was going to ask her to marry him, I didn't get the whole picture. I guess I just figured that she would stay in her house with her kids, Dad and I would stay in our house, and that they would see each other on weekends and stuff. (OK, maybe I was in denial.)

But Dad straightened me out in a hurry. Not only will we all be living together, we'll be doing it in Margie's house, since it's bigger than ours. I have to start living with strangers, and I also have to do it in a strange place! I'm losing the house I grew up in and gaining a stepmother, two stepbrothers, and a stepsister. Some trade-off.

The Bible says God comforts us in all our troubles. I hope that's true, because I feel like I've got about a million troubles right now. Dad's too busy being in love to help me, so I guess I've got no other place to turn.

Colin

Real Question

Even rock-solid believers struggle with trusting God in hard times. Don't believe that statement? Then do this experiment: start in Genesis and go straight through to Revelation. You'll find that even the giants of the faith—Abraham, Moses, David, Jeremiah, and John the Baptist, to name just a few—wavered during tough times. Funny, but it doesn't matter how much a person claims to believe in the truth of the Bible. You might even have big chunks of God's Word *memorized.* But when the roof caves in, what you need is the peace found in God.

What do you think of Colin's situation? Have you got anything in your life that's similar? What are some things that *don't* work when you're troubled and anxious?

Real Answer

In Matthew 5:4, Jesus says to his followers that "Those who mourn . . . will be comforted."

Is that true? Does Jesus really make good on his pledge?

Maybe the greatest test case of this promise is the apostle Paul. If the New Testament book of Second Corinthians is any indication, his entire life after meeting Christ was one gigantic crisis. Consider the following admissions and descriptions:

> *I think you ought to know, dear brothers and sisters, about the trouble we went through in the province of Asia. We were crushed and completely overwhelmed, and we thought we would never live through it. In fact, we expected to die.*
>
> 2 Corinthians 1:8-9

We are pressed on every side by troubles ... We are perplexed ... We are hunted down.

2 Corinthians 4:8-9

We patiently endure troubles and hardships and calamities of every kind. We have been beaten, been put in jail, faced angry mobs, worked to exhaustion, endured sleepless nights, and gone without food.

2 Corinthians 6:4-5

I have lived with weariness and pain ... Often I have shivered with cold, without enough clothing to keep me warm. Then, besides all this, I have the daily burden of how the churches are getting along.

2 Corinthians 11:27-28

Whew! Just reading that abbreviated list of troubles (2 Corinthians mentions many others) is enough to make a person want to lie down! How in the world could Paul keep going? *Why* in the world would he want to? What was his secret?

He tells us in the passage cited above: "God ... comforts us in all our troubles so that we can comfort others" (2 Corinthians 1:3-4). These weren't just mere words to Paul. It was a reality he had experienced first-hand, in countless uncomfortable times.

That same experience, if we dare believe the promise of Jesus, can be ours too. God stands ready to meet us in our time of darkness and doubt. Comfort might come through the encouragement of a friend, or the lifting of a trial, or the supernatural peace of God through prayer. But we have the promise that it *will* come.

REAL YOU

Because I have God's assurance of comfort, in times of trouble, I will do the following:

_____

_____

_____

_____

_____

_____

_____

_____

_____

_____

_____

Some friends I can comfort and some specific and practical ways I can show comfort are:

_____

_____

_____

_____

_____

_____

_____

_____

_____

_____

_____

_____

_____

Xalted

Rock of Israel

If you were looking for body comfort, you probably wouldn't look for a rock upon which to rest. But if you were looking for soul comfort, you *would* want the Rock—that is, Jesus Christ (Isaiah 30:29). We rest in him during hard and scary times, and in him we find protection, shelter, and comfort.

I discover the Jesus Answer when I trust completely in his answers to my prayers.

"You parents—if your children ask for a loaf of bread, do you give them a stone instead? Or if they ask for a fish, do you give them a snake? Of course not! If you sinful people know how to give good gifts to your children, how much more will your heavenly Father give good gifts to those who ask him."

Matthew 7:9-11

REAL Xpressions

Does Prayer Really Work?

During a speaker's talk on prayer, almost everybody is distracted and daydreaming. Lauren can't stop thinking about Caleb. Caleb is doing the same thing (that is, thinking nonstop about Caleb). Anna is wondering what she's going to wear to the banquet on Tuesday night. Tim is trying to remember what homework is due tomorrow. Donovan is thinking how good a Griff's burger would be. And on and on it goes.

About the only person in the room paying close attention is Colin (remember him from yesterday?). He's the guy who's dad is getting remarried. With such big, surprising, and unwelcome stuff going on his life, Colin wants some answers to his questions about prayer. If you asked him about it, here's what you might hear:

"I just want to know how this prayer thing works. I've been praying almost every day for both my parents for the last five years. Begging God that despite their divorce, they would eventually get back together. I guess I always heard that if you ask for something in Jesus' name, and you really believe, then it was pretty much guaranteed to happen. Just keep the faith.

"So this news from my Dad is totally blowing me away. It's the exact opposite of what I asked for, of what I was expecting. If I'm honest, I want to say, 'Thanks, God, but, uh, no thanks.'

"I want to know why God doesn't step in? Why doesn't he grant what I've been asking? Like that would be so hard for him. Man, it makes me wonder if prayer changes anything at all?"

Colin

REAL QUESTION

Prayer is one of the greatest mysteries of the spiritual life. Some verses make it sound like God is sitting in heaven, waiting to hear from us before he does anything (John 14:13-14), almost like he's offering us a blank check for "whatever" our hearts desire. Other passages give the idea that prayer is not so much getting God to sign off on our will as it is aligning ourselves to his agenda (Matthew 6:9-10; 1 John 5:14-15).

Poor Colin is really confused. He desperately needs some help. What's the truth about prayer? And how can God be worthy of our trust when he denies our deepest requests?

REAL ANSWER

The old cliché that God answers prayer in one of three ways is trite but true. Either he grants our requests. Or he doesn't. Or he asks us to wait.

Logically, if we're asking God for something, then we're going to be excited if he answers, "Yes." It's the "no" and the "not now" responses that we don't like.

Sometimes, as in Colin's case, the disappointing results of prayer may be due to the fact that God refuses to override the free will decisions of men. Could God have *forced* Colin's dad to come back to Colin's mom? Theoretically, yes. But practically, no. Not if he wanted to respect the right of his creatures to choose.

On other occasions, God says "no" to our requests simply because he will never do anything that is unwise. Remember Jesus' prayer in the

Garden of Gethsemane? "Father, if you are willing, please take this cup of suffering away from me." Remember what he said next? "Yet I want your will, not mine" (Luke 22:41-42). The Father's answer was no. Jesus went to the cross because it was God's wisdom and plan that the Son die for our sins. Jesus ultimately trusted in his Father's plan, for which we should be forever grateful. Without the cross, where would we be?

In times when God says no, it's important to remember that no amount of theatrics or fireworks or manipulation on our part is going to sway God. You can pout, get angry, make promises, even offer God deals. No matter. He will act only in a way that will bring him glory *and* you happiness. He will turn a deaf ear to foolish requests. He will answer yes when and only when the time is right. He will do only what is best. He is God and you're not.

Keep in mind the mind-boggling character of God: Perfect wisdom. Total goodness. Absolute love. God *never* ceases to be any of these things. What does that mean? That negative responses or delayed answers aren't because God is merciless. He isn't absent-minded. He can't be accused of being indifferent. On the contrary, God is orchestrating events and bringing situations in line with his perfect will. Even in making you endure agonizing waits and disappointing news, God is doing something good. He is building your character and strengthening your faith. And, sometimes, he is doing things "behind the scenes."

Real you

Some big things I want to trust God for are:

_____

_____

_____

_____

_____

_____

Because God is awesome and perfect in every way, I will give him veto power over all my current prayer requests. My biggest concerns just now are:

_____

_____

_____

_____

_____

_____

_____

_____

_____

_____

_____

_____

_____

_____

Xalted

Amen

The word "amen" means, literally, *firm* or *true.* Ascribed to Jesus (Revelation 3:14), this title means that Jesus is completely trustworthy and faithful. In your biggest times of trial, Jesus is reliable and dependable in ways that no one and nothing else is.

The ever-present question, "What about my future?" comes down to this: You can either rely on stuff like astrology columns and TV Tarot card readers with bad Jamaican accents, or you can put your trust in Jesus Christ.

GOD'S SOVEREIGNTY AND THE FUTURE

The Bible claims straight up that Jesus is Lord over all things, that all history and human events are moving towards a day when *everything* will find resolution and completion in him.

Do we believe that—*really* believe it? If not, what other explanations do we have? And if we *do* see Jesus as holding the past, present, and, even the future in his hands, what difference will that make in our lives today and this week and next year?

That's the focus of these final seven devotionals.

I discover the Jesus Answer when I live my life according to the purpose that Jesus has planned for me.

"For I have come down from heaven to do the will of God who sent me, not to do what I want."

John 6:38

REAL XPRESSIONS

My Purpose

The other day, I started thinking about my purpose in life. Really deep, right? In class yesterday, my English teacher mentioned a writer who gave up everything to follow his passion. We got into a discussion about doing what we feel passionate about. One guy wants to be a doctor overseas someday. Another girl wants to be a missionary. Another guy wants to write plays and run a marathon. (He'll be busy.)

That discussion stuck with me all that day. I started to realize that I had never thought about what I was passionate about. All I did was follow everyone else. I started playing guitar because my friend Elizabeth plays. Although I'm glad I learned, it wasn't my first choice of instruments. I also took a watercolor painting class because my friends Mikayla and Isabel wanted to take it.

I've always done things my older sister Autumn did. She played volleyball, she took Spanish, she worked for my dad all summer . . . so guess what I did? I don't even like volleyball, really, but everyone thinks Autumn is so cool. Besides, what else was I going to do? Sometimes I just don't know what I want!

I do know one thing. Esther (the beauty queen from the Bible) had a purpose. I've been reading her book this week. Just finished the last chapter yesterday. Esther was in the right place at the right time. Her cousin Mordecai told her that God had a purpose for her—a purpose that only she could fulfill. That's so cool! Still, Esther's job was scary. She had to face the possibility of death, but God was with her.

I've decided to really start praying about what God wants me to do. I'm also making a list of things that I really enjoy—what *I* like, not what my friends and my sister like. *I* really like working with kids. Maybe God has a purpose for me in that?

Fiona

Real Question

At some point, everyone—from high school students to college seniors to middle-aged sales people—asks the same questions that Fiona is asking herself: "Why am I here? What was I put here to do? What's my reason for being?"

Finding the answer to these questions can be a long and hard process. Which explains why a huge number of people finally give up. They just throw up their hands and settle for a job—the highest-paying one they can find. And they gut it out, often hating it, barely enduring, living for the weekends. So when Friday comes—good old T.G.I.F.— they try to make up for their unfulfilled work week with a couple of days of nonstop fun—pursuing amusement and hobbies, even as they subconsciously dread the arrival of Monday morning.

Is this anyway to live? Is this what you want for *your* future? Wouldn't you rather figure out while you're young, God's purpose for your life?

Real Answer

"God's purpose?" some protest. "No! Please! Anything but that! I've seen what happens to people who tell God, 'I'll do whatever you want.' They end up poor and dressed in out-of-date clothes, swabbing the sores of sick people in some third-world country. Not me. No way."

Is *that* what you think? If so, consider this amazing statement from the lips of Jesus: "My purpose is to give life in all its fullness" (John 10:10). "In all its fullness"—in other words, life to the max. Life overflowing. Jesus wants to give us anything *but* a dull existence.

Another verse in the New Testament says that when Jesus calls us to himself, it is for a big-time purpose: "For we are God's masterpiece. He has created us anew in Christ Jesus, so that we can do the good things he planned for us long ago" (Ephesians 2:10).

Looking for a sense of purpose? Meaning? Mission? According to this verse, the Lord has it all figured out. Like the writer, director, and producer of a universal, cosmic drama, he is orchestrating everything and everyone toward a desired end. His desire is that you will take your unique personality, gifts, abilities, opportunities, and so forth, and make a difference in this world.

God has a role chosen just for you, a part only you can play. How can you know what that part is? Ask yourself: "What is my passion? What am I good at? What activities and hobbies fill me with a deep sense of satisfaction?"

Some people wrongly think, *If I* really *enjoy something, then that probably isn't something God wants me to do,* as though God is some kind of sadist who is ticked when we're happy, and glad when we're miserable. Where on earth did we ever get such a perverse idea? God's will and our happiness are not opposites! God has arranged the world so that we experience the deepest joys *as we do his will.* The most fulfilled and effective people in the world are, first, those who have figured out what they're God-given passions are and second, those who are pursuing their passions in order to bring glory to God.

One last thing: don't buy the all-too-common lie that the only people God can use are those who sing really well, or preach with power. There are countless other ways your life can have an impact. Whether you're good at listening, serving, helping, befriending, counseling, assisting, comforting, conversing, cooking, writing, dancing, acting, fixing, or something else, add your unique talents to God's great mosaic. The end result will be your deep satisfaction and God's ultimate glory.

REAL YOU

The truths or insights
from today's study that
encourage me the most are:

_____

_____

_____

_____

_____

_____

_____

_____

Some of my passions are as follows:

_____

_____

_____

_____

_____

_____

_____

_____

_____

_____

Xalted

Gate

Jesus identified himself not
only as the good *shepherd* who
comes in order that his flock might experience life in all its fullness, but also as
the *gate* (John 10:7). In other words, he is the
doorway to the best kind of life. We can dink
around looking in a million places for purpose and ful-
fillment, but it is only through Christ that will we find what
our souls most deeply crave.

I discover the Jesus Answer when I actively look to confirm God's will for the choices and decisions I make.

"My nourishment comes from doing the will of God, who sent me, and from finishing his work."

John 4:34

REAL Xpressions

Looking for Answers

You might want to call me the Ann Landers of the Ridgedale Community Church youth group. I mean everyone I know comes to me for advice. Why? I'm not really sure. Maybe it's because I'm a bit more serious than most of my friends. Maybe it's because I get straight A's and I study a lot. Maybe it's because they know I read my Bible and answer lots of questions in Sunday school. (Which I do, but I don't really advertise it.)

For whatever reason, they come to me with all their problems, looking for answers. Just listen to what came my way last week:

My best friend Jessica is agonizing over her relationship with her boyfriend Mark. Should she break up or not? Things certainly aren't terrible, but they're not great either. What would God want her to do?

Carmen doesn't know what to do. She's been hanging out with Joey, who's kinda wild, and now he wants the two of them to be an "official" couple. What would her friends at church think about that?

My buddy Gregg needs to make a choice between enrolling at the local community college or looking for a job. His mom is really putting the pressure on. He needs an answer! Like immediately!

They all want to know what God wants them to do. How should I know? I have about as good a connection to God as they do! I'm not really clear on this God's will deal, either. So I just nod, try to look wise, and tell them I'll pray for them.

What else can I do?

Minda

REAL QUESTION

This has to be one of the most commonly-asked questions by those who claim to be followers of Jesus: "How can I know the will of God (that is, what God wants me to do)?"

Is it just a big guessing game? Are we totally on our own? Or does the Lord give us help and guidance?

What big decisions are you struggling with right now? What's your process for trying to figure out the direction God wants you to go?

REAL answer

Five times in only four chapters of his biography of Christ, the apostle John records Jesus speaking explicitly about something called the "will of God" (see John 4:34; 5:30; 6:38-39; 7:17; see also Mark 3:35). God had a definite, individualized mission for Jesus while he was on earth. And most Christians believe, based on verses like Colossians 1:9, that God has a unique plan for each of us too.

Someone has estimated that 90% of God's will has already been revealed to us in the pages of the Bible. For instance, we know that tomorrow when we wake up, we are supposed to: make it our goal to please God (1 Corinthians 10:31); trust God in every situation (2 Corinthians 5:7); avoid getting obsessed with stuff that doesn't matter (Colossians 3:2); act as God's representatives (2 Corinthians 5:20); avoid raunchy conversations (Ephesians 4:29); show kindness to people (Ephesians 4:32); avoid sexual immorality (1 Thessalonians 4:3); and pray about everything instead of worrying about anything (Philippians 4:6-7).

The difficulties come when we are wrestling with choices like the students in the situations above. In those times, it is helpful to remember a series of C's.

First, there's **consultation** (that is, with God). In other words, prayer. When we don't know what to do, our first response should be to ask the Lord for guidance (Joshua 9:14-15; James 1:5-8). Second, there's **counsel.** Getting feedback from godly, trusted, experienced mentors is just plain smart (see Proverbs 15:22). Third, there is everyday **common sense.** God has given you a brain. Use it! For example, it's *probably* not God's will that you become a jockey if you're 5'11" and weigh 170 pounds. We always have the help of **circumstances.** Some people call these open doors or sovereign "God things" (Romans 8:28; Ecclesiastes 7:13-14). You don't want to get overly mystical, but you also shouldn't totally discount out-of-the-blue phone calls or the unexpected events. It's true what they say: God moves in mysterious ways! Fifth, is the important element of **conviction** (some call it **conscience**). As we prayerfully consider potential courses of action, we begin to get a gut feeling about one option or a wrong feeling about another. Related to this is the stronger sense of leading some call **compulsion** (Acts 20:22; Romans 8:14). This is where you feel strongly pulled in one direction. Another help is **contentment** (Colossians 3:15) in which one course of action feels so right and fulfilling. This often morphs into what some call the state of **confirmation,** in which wise people and positive results affirm your choice. The point is to use all these resources to come to a **consensus.**

God's will isn't a set of blueprints that just drops out of the sky. It's more like a scroll that the Father, Son, and Holy Spirit unroll for us just a little bit each day, as we pursue God and his agenda. The good news is that God wants you to discover and do his will, even more than you do.

Real You

The specific decisions I'm
wrestling with today are:

_____

_____

_____

_____

_____

_____

_____

_____

_____

_____

_____

_____

_____

Using the C's above, I can make the following statements about how I think God is leading me:

_____

_____

_____

_____

_____

_____

_____

_____

_____

_____

_____

_____

Xalted

Bright Morning Star

Stars illuminate the darkness, giving light. As the so-called "bright morning star" (Revelation 22:16), Jesus shines his truth into our lives. He's the light of the world (John 8:12; 9:5) who never fails to show us the way to go. And, unlike horoscopes and astrological charts, the One who created the stars can be trusted to help determine our future.

I discover the Jesus Answer when I accept the second chance I receive through Jesus' grace and forgiveness.

At that moment the Lord turned and looked at Peter. Then Peter remembered that the Lord had said, "Before the rooster crows tomorrow morning, you will deny me three times." And Peter left the courtyard, crying bitterly.

Luke 22:61-62

REAL XPRESSIONS

Coming Back

I don't think I've ever been this nervous in my entire life. I'm about to step foot in church for the first time since having my baby and putting her up for adoption. It's going to be a big—make that a *huge*—first step. I have no idea how people are going to react to me, if they'll totally ignore me or what. I know all the people there. I mean I was brought up in that church. I was baptized there. I won the Bible memory contest there when I was eight. My family and I have always attended that church.

But now it feels totally weird. Most of the people there know what happened. Some have been really kind and supportive of me during my pregnancy and after the birth. One woman even came to visit me at the hospital after the baby was born. Others, though, I've heard (bad news travels fast) are really mad at me and probably won't speak to me.

It's so strange. I could have had an abortion, you know? Not that I *would* do that—I don't believe in it. But I know two girls at church who have done that, and so nobody knows their dirty little secret. How unfair is that? They do something wrong, and then they do an even worse thing to cover it up. And so they're able to keep this perfect little image, you know? I just figured two wrongs don't make a right. I didn't want to, you know, add any more guilt to my life. But I'll tell you this, having everyone know my dirty laundry sure doesn't make my future any easier. I did right in the end, but I gotta tell you, it hasn't been fun.

Briana

REAL QUESTION

Maybe your failures aren't as dramatic or as public as Briana's, but everyone is guilty of making wrong choices. And then comes the tough task of trying to get back on the right track.

It's a tough situation to be in. You feel shaky. Uncertain. Strange voices fill your head: "Don't blow it!" or "Why try? You screwed up before—you'll do it again."

Is it worth it? Is it possible to overcome a foolish past? Can we recover our good reputation?

In light of past mistakes, how can we look to the future with any hope?

REAL answer

Consider the Bible character Peter. He was a rough and tough fisherman, given to big talk and even bigger screwups.

The guy was forever making and then breaking promises, constantly messing up in critical situations. But Jesus never stopped loving Peter or believing in him. Check out the amazing scene in John 21. Picture yourself right there. The apostles are fishing when the resurrected Christ suddenly appears on the beach. He first guides them to a gigantic school of fish. Then a big fish dinner takes place, and though no one saw it coming, it becomes clear that Jesus has set this whole thing up for Peter's benefit. The entire scene, right down to the distinctive aroma of the charcoal fire and the three sets of questions ("Do you love me? . . . Do you love me? . . . Do you love me?"), is basically a rewinding of history to the recent night when Peter had cursed the very name of Christ three times. Wow. Imagine that. After the spectacular failure of denying even knowing Jesus, Peter is being given yet another chance to come back and get it right.

And history records that he did. He proved his love for Jesus by traveling the world with boldness, telling others of Christ, telling his own story of encountering the God of second and third—and thousandth—chances.

This can be your story too. No matter what you've done. No matter how many times you've failed, God pursues you with infinite patience and wants you to catch a glimpse of what your life can be when you let him love you, fill you, lead you, change you, and use you.

Will you let him forgive you, restore you, and recommission you to his service?

REAL YOU

Based on what I read of
Jesus in the Gospels, here
is what I think he might say
to me at my worst moments of
failure:

_____

_____

_____

_____

_____

_____

_____

_____

_____

_____

_____

_____

_____

Some of the "Briana's" in my life right now that I can show grace and compassion to are:

_____

_____

_____

_____

_____

_____

_____

_____

_____

_____

_____

_____

_____

_____

_____

_____

_____

_____

_____

_____

Χalted

The Good Shepherd

No matter how tough or cool
we think we are, the fact remains
that we are vulnerable creatures. Failure and criticism hurt, wounding us all
the way to the innermost parts of our souls. It
is a comfort to know that Jesus is the one who
watches over our souls (John 10:11-15). Only when we
hide in his absolute acceptance and love, only when we know
that he will never give up on us, do we find the strength and motiva-
tion to live as God intended.

I discover the Jesus Answer when I understand his love for me despite my weaknesses and shortcomings.

"My gracious favor is all you need. My power works best in your weakness."

2 Corinthians 12:9

REAL Xpressions

Dealt a Bad Hand?

I'm a tenth grader at Lincoln High, and I have to admit I hate school. With a passion. From day one, back in Miss Cooper's kindergarten class (I couldn't even find my own name), I've struggled in school. I have always had trouble getting my assignments straight, getting them done, and turning them in. It didn't matter so much in grade school and junior high—the teachers there give you a lot of slack—but it is killing me in high school. What's so frustrating is that I know the material, I know it cold! But when it comes down to taking the test, I get nervous and make stupid mistakes.

Well, after yet another conference with the guidance counselor, my parents decided to have me tested. This week I was assessed by a psychologist and a doctor (talk about feeling like a freak). Now everyone has a reason for why I do so poorly. I have Attention Deficit Disorder. No one really knows what causes this, only that the brains of those with ADD have trouble organizing and processing information.

The good news, so the doctors say, is that it doesn't mean I'm dumb. Far from it! The smarts are there. In fact in some subjects, I even tested at the college level. The problem is physiological, medical. And, according to the doctor, it's treatable with medication.

That's supposed to make me feel better. But I don't see it that way. Basically, no matter how they try to spin it, they're saying I'm defective. Like I need to be parking in the handicapped spaces at the mall. Bottom line, my brain doesn't function right. And so now I have this great choice:

drug myself up every day and be a zombie who makes good grades, or skip the medication and kiss my academic future good-bye. Gee, God, thanks a lot!

Anton

REAL QUESTION

Anton's reaction is understandable. Who wants to get news like that?

Yet, if we're objective and honest, everyone has liabilities, limitations, and handicaps of one kind or another. You may not be diagnosed with ADD, but you have some shortcoming or weakness in your life. Nobody in this world (despite appearances) has it all together. Nobody has a perfect life.

What is that thing you hate about yourself—that trait or inability or problem that causes you to think, *Man, what a raw deal! Why did God have to make me like this?* What would you change if you had a magic wand?

More importantly, how do we find the courage to face the future when things right now aren't so hot?

REAL ANSWER

The tendency is to think Jesus had it easy. After all, he had all power. He was God in the flesh. He even said it himself, if he wanted he could call on a whole army of angels to come to his aid.

But have you ever really looked at all the facts? Consider that Jesus came into the world with a dark cloud of scandal hanging over him. *We* know all about "the virgin birth." All his relatives and townspeople knew that if you did the math concerning wedding dates and birth dates, Jesus was, well, "early." And his parents? Not prominent or wealthy. Not able to get him in the greatest schools. When he finally did begin his public ministry, his siblings wanted to commit him to a mental asylum and his neighbors wanted to kill him (see Mark 3:21 and Luke 4:28-30). If not for the financial support of a few women and friends, Jesus would never have had two cents to rub together. Then you come to that bizarre scene where Jesus is so worked up, so scared by what God was asking him to do, he's literally sweating blood.

Jesus "had it easy"? No way. When you stop and think about it, neither did any of the rest of the real people whose stories are told in the Bible. Moses had a speech impediment. David was on the short side, "vertically challenged" we might say today. Peter lacked a formal education. Paul had some mysterious, nagging ailment or problem that he called simply, "a thorn in the flesh."

The point is that Jesus understands our weaknesses and inadequacies. Why? Because he faced a boatload of liabilities himself.

So next time you feel like you've been given a raw deal by God, try to remember these truths. Everybody has issues. Individually, we have huge gaps, but with God's grace and power, together with other believers, we can maximize our strengths and minimize our weaknesses. We can cover for each other, which is the beauty of the Church.

REAL YOU

The things about myself that I don't like and wish I could change are:

_____

_____

_____

_____

_____

_____

_____

_____

_____

The next time I start feeling sorry for myself, or start feeling like I don't have what it takes, I will:

_____

_____

_____

_____

_____

_____

_____

_____

_____

_____

_____

_____

_____

_____

_____

_____

_____

_____

_____

_____

_____

_____

Xalted

Lord God Almighty

Someone has said that when we have a little God, we have big problems, but when we have a big God, we have little problems. Seeing (and remembering) God's greatness is essential for having a right perspective on our problems. Take time to reflect on the truth that Jesus is not a mild-mannered carpenter from Nazareth or a meek little Jewish rabbi. No, he is the Lord God Almighty (Revelation 15:3). *Nothing* is too hard for him.

I discover the Jesus Answer when I put aside my worries and trust in him.

"So don't worry about tomorrow, for tomorrow will bring its own worries. Today's trouble is enough for today."

Matthew 6:34

REAL Xpressions

Stressed Out

Sometimes I get so mad when I hear people go on and on about the "millennium generation" this and the "millennium generation" that. Like we're supposed to have all the answers for the future. At times, I feel like the weight of the future is resting right on my shoulders! As if I need any more pressure.

Take this weekend, for example. The SATs are Saturday morning. I've already taken them twice and I've only done slightly better than average. My parents keep reminding me of the score I'll "probably need to get into the schools of your choice" (or, more accurately, the school—singular—of *their* choice). It's crazy! I feel like if I don't do well this time, I'll end up working at McDonald's all my life. That should make my parents really happy.

Then, there's the auditions coming up for the school musical. I really, really want to be in the show this year, but there's a lot of competition. (A lot!) I can't make up my mind as to which monologue I want to use in the audition. I'm not even sure when I can memorize it. I've got two major projects due next week and I haven't done *anything* on either one. (Mainly because I've been studying for the SAT. Ugh!) And I have to baby-sit for Mrs. Brady's two hyper kids after the test.

Which brings me to another sore topic—getting a "real" summer job! (Translation: not just baby-sitting.) If I hear my mom nag me one more time about now's the time to start looking for a job . . . I'm going to lose it! It isn't enough that she keeps bringing me home these applications. I just don't have the time right now to even think about it, much less fill out all those applications!

Then my mom has the nerve to ask me why I look so stressed out. Gee, I don't know ...

Jillian

REAL QUESTION

Take a few moments and list all the benefits that come from worry. Let's see ... there's the encouraging truth that fretting doesn't change a thing. Ever. You can stress out all you want, and guess what, you'll be right where you were when you started.

What else? Hmmm ... how about the comforting fact that anxiety devours our emotional energy and depletes our spiritual resources with the result that we become mostly unproductive in the other areas of life. Everything else—relationships, academic or athletic performance—suffers when we agonize feverishly over our problems. Most medical researchers are now convinced that excessive worry can even wreak havoc on us physically, resulting in everything from zits to ulcers, headaches and weight gain—perhaps even being a leading cause of depression, heart attacks, and strokes!

Isn't there a better way to handle trials and stress than just freaking out?

REAL ANSWER

The way we Christians sometimes live our lives, you'd think everything in the world depended on us. We rush around, we get up early and stay up late, we try so hard, we do so much, but we rest and pray so little. When you think about it, doesn't it seem like a contradiction in terms for a follower of the Prince of Peace to be a nervous wreck?

Jesus had some intriguing things to say to those who are restless and worn out from anxiety. In addition to the classic passage mentioned above, here are some more nuggets of truth:

- In Matthew 11:28-29, to a big crowd of people: "Come to me, all of you who are weary and carry heavy burdens, and I will give you rest. Take my yoke upon you. Let me teach you, because I am humble and gentle, and you will find rest for your souls."
- In Mark 6:31: "Then Jesus said [to his closest disciples], 'Let's get away from the crowds for a while and rest.' There were so many people coming and going that Jesus and his apostles didn't even have time to eat."
- One who walked with Jesus said this in 1 Peter 5:7: "Give all your worries and cares to God, for he cares about what happens to you."

The thing that leaps out at you in these statements is Jesus' deep concern for worried and weary people. He longs to deliver us from the heaviness of trying to carry the world on our shoulders. When the pressures and stresses of life have zapped your strength, when concerns about the future threaten to overwhelm you, the temptation is to push harder and worry even more. That's precisely when we need to stop and listen to the still, small voice of Christ say, "Time out! Pull back. Turn off your mind for a while. Turn over your concerns to me. I care about you more than you know, and I'm big enough to deal with your issues."

Maybe author Charlotte Bronte said it best when she admitted, "I try to avoid looking forward or backward, and try to keep looking upward." That's what we're talking about here. Lifting your eyes and your prayers up to heaven, to the only one who can really give the help you need.

REAL YOU

My biggest worries just
now are these:

_____

_____

_____

_____

_____

_____

_____

_____

_____

_____

_____

_____

_____

Because Jesus commands me to trust and rest in him (rather than worry), when I feel my heart starting to race in the face of a new concern, I will take the following steps:

_____

_____

_____

_____

_____

_____

_____

_____

_____

_____

_____

_____

_____

_____

Xalted

Prince of Peace

That great messianic prophecy of Isaiah (see Isaiah 9:6) refers to Jesus as the "Prince of Peace." What great news for those whose insides are tied up in knots! Jesus doesn't just offer us a little bit of comfort, or a few consoling words. He offers us himself—ultimate peace, peace without end. Got peace?

I discover the Jesus Answer when I believe with confidence that heaven will be my eternal home.

"And just as my Father has granted me a Kingdom, I now grant you the right to eat and drink at my table in that Kingdom. And you will sit on thrones, judging the twelve tribes of Israel."

Luke 22:29-30

REAL Xpressions

Almost Heaven

We had been here for three days and it still didn't seem real to me. An all-expenses-paid week in the Cayman Islands with my best friend, Tami, splashing about in the blue waters of the Caribbean, soaking up rays on a private beach outside a deluxe villa that looks like something out of *Architectural Digest.* Me, Kelli, the girl who has never gone on a vacation that doesn't require a camper or a makeshift cookstove.

As we sat eating some kind of exotic fish at this super trendy restaurant, I asked Tami one more time, "OK, tell me again how your dad gets this deal?" She laughed. "Well, it's not really 'a deal.' His investment firm does a ton of banking business here, and they already had their company Learjet. So then they thought, 'why not get a place, instead of always staying in hotels?' It just made sense. So now the principal owners and their families get to use the place if nothing else is going on."

Can you believe that anyone can be that lucky? The scenery was so incredibly beautiful, I couldn't help but gush as we left the restaurant, "It's like a little slice of heaven."

So there we sat, lounging right out by the water's edge, just taking it all in. It was getting close to sunset and the sky was on fire with breathtaking patches of red and orange. A gentle sea breeze was blowing. I was almost asleep when Tami broke the silence. "I wonder if heaven *will* be like this?"

"Hmmm. I don't know. Sometimes I wonder if there's really such a place."

Kelli

REAL QUESTION

Wow. That story is almost enough to make you want to pack your bags and head to the beach!

But it also raises the profound question of eternity, of life beyond this life. In these pages we've already talked about the reality of a place called hell. What about heaven? Is there such a place? What did Jesus say?

This isn't just a religious or academic question. Author C. S. Lewis has correctly observed: "We are very shy nowadays of even mentioning heaven. We are afraid of the jeer about 'pie in the sky,' and of being told that we are trying to 'escape' from the duty of making a happy world here and now . . . But either there is 'pie in the sky' or there is not. If there is not, then Christianity is false, for this doctrine is woven into its whole fabric. If there is, then this truth, like any other, must be faced . . ."

REAL ANSWER

We do not have to dig through the New Testament for hard-to-find evidence of paradise. The statements are there. Lewis is right. The doctrine of heaven "is woven into [the] whole fabric" of Christianity. Consider:

Jesus made numerous references to heaven. He often told stories suggesting and implying that heaven is a real place, not the result of a lot of wishful thinking. He frequently mentioned his "Father in heaven" and in, perhaps *the* most famous statement on the subject, he said, "There are many rooms in my Father's home, and I am going to prepare a place for you. If this were not so, I would tell you plainly. When everything is ready, I will come and get you, so that you will always be with me where I am" (John 14:2–3).

Not only did Jesus promise believers they would get to enter this eternal residence (Luke 13:24), calling them "citizens" of heaven (Luke 10:20), he further promised his faithful followers they would receive "treasure" and "rewards" one day in heaven (Mark 10:21; Luke 6:23; 12:33; 16:9).

The other New Testament writers add a lot of other facts. Heaven is described as a place of joy (Colossians 1:5), light (James 1:17), intense praise (Revelation 5:13), and celebration (Luke 15:7). Revelation 21 and 22 depict in some detail a spectacular kingdom where the forgiven children of God say good-bye forever to mourning, sadness, and pain. Other heavenly glimpses in Revelation are so awesome and vivid as to almost make the hair stand up on your neck.

So, forget the old idea that we will sit around on clouds strumming on harps of gold, or that heaven will be like an eternal version of a really dull church service. The biblical picture is one of breathtaking joy and ecstasy, not of boredom. Heaven will be a place of unsurpassed beauty and wonder—mostly because we will be in the very presence of the living God. We will walk and talk with him, face-to-face.

Again, C. S. Lewis, in his book *The Weight of Glory,* says it so well:

> "The door on which we have been knocking all our lives will open at last. Apparently, then, our lifelong nostalgia, our longing to be reunited with something in the universe from which we now feel cut off, to be on the inside of some door which we have always seen from the outside, is no mere neurotic fancy, but the truest index of our real situation. And to be at last summoned inside would be both glory and honour beyond all our merits and also the healing of that old ache."

REAL YOU

My biggest questions
about heaven are:

_____

_____

_____

_____

_____

_____

_____

_____

_____

The most surprising thing I've learned about heaven from the Bible is:

_____

_____

_____

_____

_____

_____

_____

_____

_____

_____

_____

_____

Xalted

Resurrection and Life

After the death of Lazarus, Jesus claims this title in John 11:25. Among other things, it means that he is master over death, victor over the grave, and that he holds the keys to the amazing and wonderful world to come. Have you embraced Christ as the only one who can forgive your sin and open the door to heaven?

I discover the Jesus Answer when I recognize his control over all events in my life and in the world.

"My Father has given me authority over everything."
Luke 10:22

REAL Xpressions

Is God in Control?

Not too many people keep journals anymore—especially not too many guys. But I do. I'll write for, oh, 20 or 30 minutes every morning. Just jotting down my thoughts. Whatever I'm feeling at the moment, whatever comes to mind. It helps me sort things out and get things off my chest. Like this situation:

Monday

I'm not exactly looking forward to this week. I've got a ton of stuff going on at school. A couple of big tests (and in classes where I *have* to do well . . . or else!). A pretty major project due for history. Plus with regionals coming up, I know Coach Cangelosi is going to push us really hard. I have a feeling practices will last at least half an hour longer each day . . . like I need something extra to do.

And that's just me. I know my parents are *really* concerned about my brother in the military. There's a good chance his unit might be moved even closer to the action. He's a tough guy and all that, but I worry about him too.

And if that's not enough, things in my dad's company aren't going well at all. They've downsized a couple of times already the past few years. And now, in the last several days, there's talk about another round of layoffs. Dad tries to act like he's not worried, that it'll all be OK, but I think deep down he's really sweating it. I know, if he got axed, he'd have a hard time finding a similar position around here. So that could mean moving. Oh, man, I don't even want to go there.

People talk about how the world is getting smaller all the time. You know, the "global village" and all that. I guess in a lot of ways, that's true.

Look at how a handful of terrorists can highjack and crash four planes and throw the whole world into political and even financial chaos. What if something even bigger happened? What if some nut in a far-off place got his hands on a nuke and decided to use it?

At church yesterday we sang some new praise song about God being in control. It's a pretty catchy song, but when I think about everything, I wonder, is he *really?*

Curtis

Real question

Ever play the "what if" game? That's where you let your brain run wild and you come up with every possible disaster you can think of: "What if a meteorite hits my house? What if the lunch lady is really a terrorist and puts Ebola virus in the mashed potatoes? What if I die before I get to have sex? What if a meteorite hits me on my wedding night—right before I have sex?"

Some people play this game endlessly and go in the tank. Other people take a different approach. They ask the question: "Is God really in control of the world—and my life?" And then they go to the Bible in search of answers.

Real answer

Is God in control? Is Christ Lord? Every time that question comes up in the Bible, the answer is a *big* thumbs up. Always yes! So we naturally wonder, why then does bad stuff happen left and right? When wars and accidents and natural disasters "happen" every single day, it gets pretty tough to believe that somewhere "up there" sits an all-powerful one we call the Lord.

If you didn't know better, and if all you looked at was the depressing chaos we call the world, you'd be tempted to see God, at best, as a kind of bumbling, well-meaning, but very incompetent deity. Trying hard to hold it together, but not succeeding very well.

Ah, but we do know better. Things are not what they *seem*. Things are what they *are*. And what are they? Let's let Jesus tell us:

- Matthew 11:27: "My Father has given me authority over everything" (see also Luke 10:22).
- Matthew 28:18: "I have been given complete authority in heaven and on earth."
- John 16:33: "Here on earth you will have many trials and sorrows. But take heart, because I have overcome the world."

Other New Testament passages affirm Jesus' words:

- Ephesians 1:21-22: "Now he [Jesus] is far above any ruler or authority or power or leader or anything else in this world or in the world to come. And God has put all things under the authority of Christ."
- Revelation 11:15: "The whole world has now become the kingdom of our Lord and of his Christ, and he will reign forever and ever."

This final book of the Bible also refers to God as "Sovereign Lord" (Revelation 6:10). "Sovereign" is not a word we use a lot today, but it means "having supreme power and absolute authority." It suggests the indisputable right to command obedience.

There will come a day when every knee will bow to Christ (Philippians 2:10). Meanwhile, our gracious, patient God is giving the whole world the opportunity to voluntarily proclaim him Lord, before that awesome and terrible day when they will be forced against their will to acknowledge him as King of the universe.

It's hard to trust when things are tough, but one day, like the solving of a giant, cosmic puzzle, it will all make sense. The apostle Paul put it this way: "Now we see things imperfectly as in a poor mirror, but then we will see everything with perfect clarity" (1 Corinthians 13:12).

REAL YOU

The events in my life or in the world that have caused me to question the Lord's control of all things are:

_____

_____

_____

_____

_____

_____

_____

_____

_____

_____

_____

_____

_____

_____

_____

_____

_____

_____

_____

_____

_____

_____

_____

Some practical things I can do to bolster my faith when I'm starting to feel like everything is coming unraveled are:

_____

_____

_____

_____

_____

_____

_____

_____

_____

_____

_____

χALTED

Alpha and Omega

Alpha is the first letter of the Greek alphabet; omega is the last. Thus the title "Alpha and Omega" (Revelation 1:8) means that Jesus Christ encompasses, supercedes, and sustains all things. He is before everything and after everything. He is the Creator, Savior, and Judge of the universe. Christ is *all* (Colossians 3:11). And that translates into total control over everything. Nothing—and no one—is beyond his reach. Praise him for that today!